NAMESAKES 2000

The Thirteenth Book In The Namesakes Series

A NEW and Updated photohistory of CURRENT Great-Lakes Vessels

NAMESAKES 2000

THE THIRTEENTH BOOK IN THE NAMESAKES SERIES

The Factual Story with Photographs of Currently Existing Bulk Freighters, Self-Unloaders, Tankers, Carferries, Cement Carriers and Barges. Vessels in the Great Lakes Fleet Telling the "Why" and the Meaning of Each Vessel's Name with 350 Ship Names. Cross-referenced

BY JOHN ORVILLE GREENWOOD, M.B.A.

Published by
FRESHWATER PRESS, INC.
1700 E. 13th Street, Cleveland, OH 44114 U.S.A.

OTHER PUBLICATIONS OF FRESHWATER PRESS, INC.

Greenwood's Guide to Great Lakes Shipping (Annual)
Greenwood's & Dills' Lake Boats (Annual)
The Lakeboats Calendar
Namesakes 1900 - 1909 - John O. Greenwood
Namesakes 1910 - 1919 - John O. Greenwood
Namesakes 1920 - 1929 - John O. Greenwood
Namesakes 1930 - 1955 - John O. Greenwood
Namesakes 1956 - 1980 - John O. Greenwood
Fleet Histories Series - Volume I - John O. Greenwood
Fleet Histories Series - Volume II - John O. Greenwood
Fleet Histories Series - Volume III - John O. Greenwood
Fleet Histories Series - Volume IV - John O. Greenwood
Fleet Histories Series - Volume V - John O. Greenwood
Fleet Histories Series - Volume VI - John O. Greenwood
Fleet Histories Series - Volume VII - John O. Greenwood
The Ford Fleet - C. J. Snider & M. W. Davis
Great Lakes Ships We Remember - Detroit Marine Historical Society
Great Lakes Ships We Remember II - Detroit Marine Historical Society
Great Lakes Ships We Remember III - Detroit Marine Historical Society
History of The Great Lakes - Beers (2 Volume Set)
Lore of The Lakes - Dana Thomas Bowen
Memories of the Lakes - Dana Thomas Bowen
Shipwrecks of the Lakes - Dana Thomas Bowen
Ghost Ships of the Great Lakes - Dwight Boyer
Great Stories of the Great Lakes -Dwight Boyer
True Tales of the Great Lakes - Dwight Boyer
Ships and Men of the Great Lakes - Dwight Boyer
Strange Adventures of the Great Lakes - Dwight Boyer
The Lower St. Lawrence - Ivan S. Brookes
The Honorable Peter White - Ralph Williams
Over 700 Photographs

****Current Catalog Available Upon Request••••

ISBN: 0912514-46-9
Library of Congress No. 99076458
Printed and Manufactured in the United States of America

NAMESAKES 2000 is dedicated to Jane's and my very good friends Peg and Dick Chandler, Sherry and Ray Scheetz and Winkie and John Raleigh.

"Friendship is a blessing,
and to all who have a friend,
It's one of the most precious gifts
that life could ever send."

Emily Matthews

John O. Greenwood

CONTENTS

FLEET **PAGE**

EXPLANATION and PREFACE

NAMESAKES 2000 is the thirteenth book in "The NAMESAKES Series." Briefly recapped, these are as follows:

NAMESAKES OF THE LAKES (1970) - *out of print*
NAMESAKES II (1973) former ships: 1940-1972 period, *out of print*
NEW NAMESAKES OF THE LAKES (1975) current ships, *out of print*
NAMESAKES 1900-1909 (1987) former ships in the 1900-1909 period
NAMESAKES 1910-1919 (1986) former ships in the 1910-1919 period
NAMESAKES 1920-1929 (1984) former ships in the 1920-1929 period
NAMESAKES 1930-1955 (1978) former ships in the 1930-1955 period, *out of print*
NAMESAKES 1956-1980 (1981) former ships in the 1956-1980 period
NAMESAKES OF THE '80's (1980) current ships, *out of print*
NAMESAKES OF THE '80's Volume Two (1984) current ships, *out of print*
NAMESAKES OF THE '90's (1991) Current ships, *out of print*
NAMESAKES 1930-1955 Revised & Enlarged (1995) former ships in the 1930-1955 period
NAMESAKES 2000 (2000) current ships

NAMESAKES 2000 is a new book for a new millennium. Many vessel ownerships and name changes have occurred in the past decade and this book chronicles them all.

Vessel names are thoroughly cross-indexed, allowing researchers easy reference to any of 177 vessels in this volume.

A special thank you is due friends who have contributed some of the ship photographs in this volume. They are: Jay Bascom, Brian Bluekamp, Rod Burdick, Rob Colwell, Brendan Groh, Jim Hoffman, "Buck" Longhurst, Gene Onchulenko, Al Sagon-King, "Sandy" Smith, Jim Sprunt, Franz Von Riedel and Wendell Wilke.

To these individuals, and others in the industry, I extend a personal thanks for helping us bring this latest volume of NAMESAKES to you.

John O. Greenwood

Motor Vessel AGAWA CANYON

OWNER:	**Algoma Central Marine**
BUILT:	Collingwood Shipyards, Collingwood, Ontario—1970
HULL NO.:	195
O. A. DIMENSIONS:	646′6″ × 72′ × 40′

Beginning its livelihood as a Great Lakes self-unloader in November, 1970, the Motor Vessel AGAWA CANYON took its name from the scenic gorge and canyon on the mainline of the owners' rail link to the north from Sault Ste. Marie, Ontario.

Agawa is the name of both the canyon and the small railroad station about one hundred-fifteen miles north of Sault Ste. Marie. The name is Ojibwan and means "sheltered place or harbor." Originally it was a name used to describe the mouth of the Agawa River which winds along the floor of the Agawa Canyon. The river is fed by numerous waterfalls and cascades in the canyon and is very scenic. Special excursion trains are run in the summer season so that tourists to the area may get a first-hand vista of the surrounding beauty.

The main line of the Algoma Central Railway follows the course of the Agawa River through the canyon providing spectacular views of the scenery in this lush forest countryside.

The Motor Vessel AGAWA CANYON was the only vessel added to the Great Lakes fleet, either Canadian or American, in 1970 that was not of the tank vessel class. The ship is shown in the St. Mary's River, West Neebish Channel on July 10, 1981.

Motor Vessel JOHN B. AIRD

OWNER:	Algoma Central Marine
BUILT:	Collingwood Shipyards, Collingwood, Ontario - 1983
HULL NO.:	224
O. A. DIMENSIONS:	730' x 75'10" x 46'6"

The namesake of this modern bulk freight self-unloader is Mr. John Black Aird, Lieutenant-Governor of the province of Ontario when the ship took his name. He was born on May 5, 1923 at Toronto, Ontario and was educated at Upper Canada College and Trinity College. He graduated from the latter in 1946 with a B.A. degree. Mr. Aird then went to Osgoode Hall and read law with Wilton & Edison until joining that firm in 1949.

Mr. Aird became a partner in Edison, Aird & Berlis in 1953. In 1974 the firm became Aird, Zimmerman & Berlis and, in 1978, Aird & Berlis. Mr. Aird was appointed the Queen's Counsel on January 1, 1960. He is also the former chairman of the board of the Algoma Central Railway and Reed Stenhouse Companies. He remains a director of numerous Canadian companies. On October 21, 1982, when the after 610' of his namesake was launched, Mr. Aird and a few other shipyard officials, together with Mr. William Davis, premier of Ontario, rode the ship off the blocks and into the wet slip to cheers of thousands.

This vessel sailed on its maiden voyage June 13, 1983 when it departed Thunder Bay, Ontario with coal for Nanticoke, Ontario delivery. It is shown downbound in the West Neebish Channel, St. Mary's River on August 12, 1986.

Motor Vessel ALGOBAY

OWNER:	Algoma Central Marine
BUILT:	Collingwood Shipyards, Collingwood, Ontario - 1978
HULL NO.:	215
O. A. DIMENSIONS:	730' x 75'10" x 46'6"
FORMER DATA:	Launched as ALGOBAY. Renamed ATLANTIC TRADER in 1994. Renamed ALGOBAY, for the second time, in 1997.

The Motor Vessel ALGOBAY was launched and christened on June 19, 1978. The familiar ALGO in this fleet was utilized in the prefix of the vessel's name and refers to the owning company, that being Algoma Central Corporation.

The suffix, BAY, refers to no specific bay, but to all the bays of the Great Lakes. Some of the more prominent bays are: Thunder Bay, Whitefish Bay, St.Louis Bay, Georgian Bay, Green Bay, Saginaw Bay and the Bay of Quinte.

The ship sailed on its maiden voyage October 25, 1978 light from Collingwood, Ontario to Stoneport,Michigan to load limestone for delivery to Sarnia, Ontario.The carrier is shown here approaching Hallett Dock #6 in Duluth, Minnesota to load a cargo of bentonite on November 6, 1985.

The reason for the vessel's renaming in 1994 was that this owner had entered into a charter of the carrier to Canada Steamship Lines that extended through 1996. They did not desire to use the ALGOBAY name during the period of that charter.

Motor Vessel ALGOCAPE (2)

OWNER:	Algoma Central Marine
BUILT:	Davie Shipbuilding, Limited, Lauzon, Quebec -1967
HULL NO.:	654
O. A. DIMENSIONS:	729'9"x 75'4" x 39'8"
FORMER DATA:	Launched as RICHELIEU (3). Given present name in 1994.

The bulk freight Motor Vessel ALGOCAPE (2) sailed on its maiden voyage April 5, 1967 from Quebec City, Quebec to Pointe Noire, Quebec, in ballast, to load iron ore pellets. The cargo was then delivered to Hamilton,Ontario.

The common vessel name prefix, ALGO, is utilized along with the word CAPE. While there is no specific cape intended in this carrier's name, it could be reasoned that Cape Gargantua might be the place closest to the company's operations over the years.

Cape Gargantua is located on Lake Superior's eastern shore, about 25 miles from Michipicoten Harbour, Ontario. That site was the original shipping point for Algoma Central in the 1899-1900 period when iron ore shipments originated inland at the Helen Mine. Shipments and receipts continue today, but ownership of the property changed to others in the spring of 1994.

The Motor Vessel ALGOCAPE (2) is shown in this photograph upbound in ballast, just above Lock #6 of the Welland Ship Canal on October 30, 1997.

Motor Vessel ALGOCEN (2)

OWNER:	Algoma Central Marine
BUILT:	Collingwood Shipyards, Collingwood, Ontario - 1968
HULL NO.:	191
O. A. DIMENSIONS:	730' x 75' x 39'8"

The Algoma Central Corporation, through the operation of its steamships and motor vessels, is credited with being the oldest Canadian bulk freight carrier in continuous operation on the Great Lakes. Four freighters were acquired in England in 1900 to form the initial steamship department.

Though its earliest vessels bore another class of names, the firm began using part of its own name for ships in the 1930's. The Motor Vessel ALGOCEN (2) carries on that tradition, using the first 4 letters of Algoma and the first 3 letters of Central.

This owner was originally incorporated August 11, 1899 as the Algoma Central Railway Company. The name was changed to Algoma Central & Hudson Bay Railway on May 23, 1901, then to Algoma Central Railway in the mid-1960's. It became Algoma Central Corporation in 1990.

This Seaway-sized bulk freighter is shown below while downbound in the West Neebish Channel, St. Mary's River, on August 28, 1982.

Steamer ALGOGULF (2)

OWNER:	Algoma Central Marine
BUILT:	Canadian Vickers Shipyards, Limited, Montreal, Quebec - 1961
HULL NO.:	276
O. A. DIMENSIONS:	730' x 75' x 39'
FORMER DATA:	Launched as J. N. McWATTERS (2). Renamed SCOTT MISENER (4) in 1991. Given present name in 1994.

The Steamer ALGOGULF (2) set a St. Lawrence Seaway iron ore cargo record on August 12, 1961 when it loaded 24,316 gross tons at the port of Sept-Iles, Quebec for delivery to Cleveland,Ohio. This record stood until September 9, 1963 when it was broken by another carrier.

This vessel name was chosen in specific reference to the eastern end of the St. Lawrence River which is commonly called the GULF of St. Lawrence. From the time of passing Quebec City, Quebec, the river gradually widens steadily until reaching Pointe des Monts where it is about 30 miles wide. Flowing east towards the Atlantic Ocean, the river increases in width until Anticosti Island separates it into the Jacques Cartier Passage to the north and the Gaspe Passage to the south.

Through these passages, the St. Lawrence is a mighty corridor which opens the heartland of North America to the commerce of the world.This region's namesake is shown passing downbound with grain from Duluth/Superior for a St. Lawrence River port, in the Welland Ship Canal between Locks #2 and #3, on October 29, 1997.

Motor Vessel ALGOISLE

OWNER: Algoma Central Marine
BUILT: Verolme Cork Shipyard Limited, Cork, Ireland - 1963
HULL NO.: 662
O. A. DIMENSIONS: 730' x 75' x 39'3"
FORMER DATA: Launched as SILVER ISLE. Given present name in 1994.

Commissioning of the Motor Vessel ALGOISLE for Great Lakes service took place on May 8, 1963 at Sept-Iles, Quebec after the vessel had made a trans-Atlantic voyage from Ireland under its own power. The carrier was the first large Great Lakes bulk freighter to be constructed with all accommodations aft and was also the first large, modern ship to be built from the keel up at an overseas shipyard.

This vessel was one of two acquired from the Pioneer Fleet, owned by James Richardson & Sons of Winnipeg, Manitoba, when Great Lakes Bulk Carriers was dissolved in the spring of 1994. It, too, had a very colorful paint scheme as a Pioneer vessel, that being white, yellow and orange. This scheme was incorporated to match Richardson's grain elevator markings.

Algoma Central managers decided to retain the ISLE portion of the vessel's former name because it easily identified the renamed carrier and it was easily pronounced. The common prefix, ALGO, was again utilized. The ALGOISLE is shown in this photograph downbound below Lock 8 of the Welland Ship Canal on November 15, 1998.

Motor Vessel ALGOLAKE

OWNER:	**Algoma Central Marine**
BUILT:	Collingwood Shipyards, Collingwood, Ontario - 1977
HULL NO.:	211
O. A. DIMENSIONS:	730' x 75' x 46'6"

The modern self-unloading Motor Vessel ALGOLAKE sailed on its maiden voyage April 17, 1977, light from Owen Sound, Ontario to Stoneport, Michigan to load limestone for Sarnia, Ontario delivery. It had left Collingwood for sea trials on April 16th and moored at Owen Sound for minor adjustments that evening before going into service.

This large carrier honors the owning company in the prefix of its name, ALGO being the common prefix used in the 1970's for ship names in the fleet. The specific namesake is the Great Lakes. No one of the five is singled out because this vessel travels on all of them. Rather, the entire system of Great Lakes waters is honored.

The Great Lakes comprise Lakes Superior, Michigan, Huron, Erie and Ontario and cover an area of 94,710 square miles. From the level of Lake Superior to the level of Lake Ontario, commerce descends 357 feet. Below Lake Ontario, through the St. Lawrence River, commerce makes another substantial drop to sea level below Montreal, Quebec.

The Motor Vessel ALGOLAKE is shown above while downbound in the West Neebish Channel, St. Mary's River on June 5, 1986.

Motor Vessel ALGOMARINE

OWNER:	Algoma Central Marine
BUILT:	Davie Shipbuilding, Limited, Lauzon, Quebec - 1968
HULL NO.:	665
O. A. DIMENSIONS:	730' x 75' x 39'8"
FORMER DATA:	Launched as the bulk freighter LAKE MANITOBA. Given present name in 1987. Converted to a self-unloader at Canadian Shipbuilding & Engineering Limited, Port Weller, Ontario in 1989.

The bulk freight Motor Vessel ALGOMARINE set two cargo records during her first full season of operation by loading 1,001,130 bushels of corn at South Chicago, Illinois on April 25, 1969 and by loading 27,170 gross tons of iron ore at Port Arthur, Ontario on July 4, 1969 for delivery to Cleveland, Ohio. The records were shortlived, however, with both having been surpassed by other vessels that fall.

With the fleet prefix ALGO, the specific namesake reference in this carrier's name is to the entire MARINE staff of the Algoma Central Corporation. Included are not only the shipboard personnel, but also the general office group located in Sault Ste. Marie, Ontario and the operating group located in Port Colborne, Ontario.

The Motor Vessel ALGOMARINE is shown in this photograph on April 23, 1989 while unloading a limestone cargo at Sombra, Ontario.

Motor Vessel ALGONORTH

OWNER:	Algoma Central Marine
BUILT:	Upper Clyde Shipbuilders, Limited, Govan, Scotland - 1971
HULL NO.:	101-G
O. A. DIMENSIONS:	729'9" x 75'2" x 42'11"
FORMER DATA:	Launched as TEMPLE BAR. Lengthened 202' at Jurong Shipyard, Limited, Singapore, Singapore and renamed LAKE NIPIGON in 1977. Renamed LAKETON (2) in 1984. Renamed LAKE NIPIGON, for the second time, in 1986. Given present name in 1987.

The Motor Vessel ALGONORTH is a bulk freighter which was originally constructed for use on saltwater. The reconstruction noted above gave the ship much greater carrying capacity, but meant that it became strictly a Great Lakes-Seaway trading vessel.

When this carrier was renamed in 1987, it was part of a group of six vessels which were renamed. All of those names, with one exception, were chosen using the general fleet prefix, ALGO, with the suffix in the ship name being the specific namesake reference. NORTH, in this context, refers to the railways's route north from Sault Ste. Marie, Ontario.

The Motor Vessel ALGONORTH is shown in this photograph while downbound in the West Neebish Channel, St. Mary's River, on June 9, 1990.

Motor Vessel ALGONTARIO

OWNER: Algoma Central Marine
BUILT: Schlieker-Werft, Hamburg, West Germany - 1960
HULL NO.: 536-Schlieker-Werft & 692-Davie
O.A. DIMENSIONS: 730' x 75'9" x 40'2"
FORMER DATA: Launched as RUHR ORE. Renamed CARTIERCLIFFE HALL in 1976. Lengthened 184' and widened 1'8" with new forebody at Davie Shipbuilding, Limited, Lauzon, Quebec in 1977. Renamed WINNIPEG (4) in 1988. Given present name in 1994.

The entire after house of the Motor Vessel ALGONTARIO was rebuilt following a disastrous fire on Lake Superior in June 1979 when the vessel was a member of the Hall Fleet. The ship returned to service in the spring of 1980 after rebuilding at Port Arthur Shipbuilding Company in Thunder Bay, Ontario.

Carrying capacity of this bulk freighter is 29,100 gross tons when loaded to midsummer draft of 28'3". It combined the usual prefix, ALGO, with the province of ONTARIO to form the vessel name. Ontario is the home province of this corporation, with headquarters being located in Sault Ste. Marie. Marine operations are centered in St. Catharines, Ontario.

Ontario has a population of just over 10 million and a land area of 334,092 square miles. Of this area, 106,806,000 acres is forest land! The Motor Vessel ALGONTARIO is shown while downbound in Little Rapids Cut, St. Mary's River, on August 5, 1995 with a cargo of grain from Thunder Bay, Ontario destined for delivery to Quebec City, Quebec.

Motor Vessel ALGOPORT

OWNER:	**Algoma Central Marine**
BUILT:	Collingwood Shipyards, Collingwood, Ontario - 1979
HULL NO.:	217
O. A. DIMENSIONS:	658′ x 75′10½″ x 46′6″

The Motor Vessel ALGOPORT sailed on its maiden voyage from Collingwood, Ontario to Calcite, Michigan to load a cargo of limestone for Spragge, Ontario delivery on August 27, 1979. It then entered the usual trade routes of the fleet.

Namesake of this vessel is the city of Port Colborne, Ontario. The usual prefix, ALGO, precedes the suffix, PORT. Port Colborne was chosen because the operating headquarters of the vessels is there. This move was made because of the proximity to the Welland Ship Canal through which most ships of the fleet pass continually.

Port Colborne was first settled in 1832 when it was called Gravelly Bay, but soon was named Port Colborne by Mr. W. H. Merritt in honor of Sir John Colborne, then governor of Canada. It was incorporated as a village in 1870 and as a city in 1966. It is served by the Canadian National Railway system, two highways and is at the southern extremity of the Welland Ship Canal on Lake Erie. Two grain elevators and a large quarry are located there and a third grain elevator is located in the area known as Humberstone. This city's namesake is shown while downbound in the West Neebish Channel, St. Mary's River on August 25, 1982.

Motor Vessel ALGORAIL (2)

OWNER:	Algoma Central Marine
BUILT:	Collingwood Shipyards, Collingwood, Ontario - 1968
HULL NO.:	189
O. A. DIMENSIONS:	640'5" x 72'3" x 40'

The Motor Vessel ALGORAIL (2)'s name comes from the corporate name of the owner when the ship was built. The self-unloader is shown above while downbound in the West Neebish Channel, St. Mary's River on August 2, 1982.

While this owner was initially a railway with steamers in support services, by the 1970's the railway was loosing money badly and it was the steamship operations, plus real estate, that allowed the firm to grow and prosper. The rail line was eventually sold in early 1995.

The railway was built northward from Sault Ste. Marie, Ontario. It operated 56 miles by 1903, but expansion to Hudson Bay never came about. Rather, the line was completed to Hearst, Ontario and served the vast natural resources of the wilderness area through which it operated. Sintered iron ore from the Helen Mine on the Michipicoten Branch was a major commodity for the railway from its inception, but that dwindled to nothing once the mine was closed. Iron ore, coal and limestone are now brought into Algoma Steel, Inc. in Sault Ste. Marie almost exclusively by vessels of this fleet.

Steamer ALGORIVER

OWNER:	Algoma Central Marine
BUILT:	Canadian Vickers Shipyards, Limited, Montreal, Quebec - 1960
HULL NO.:	275
O.A. DIMENSIONS:	722'6" x 75' x 39'
FORMER DATA:	Launched as JOHN A. FRANCE (2). Given present name in 1994.

The bulk freight Steamer ALGORIVER had the distinction of setting the Great Lakes cargo record for flax during its second season of operation when it took on board 835,195 bushels of that commodity at Fort William, Ontario. The vessel departed the upper lake port on November 14, 1961 and delivered the cargo to Port Colborne, Ontario. The record still stands.

With usage of the nearly universal name prefix ALGO, this carrier's namesake reference is to the St. Mary's RIVER which connects Lake Superior to the north with Lake Huron to the south. The world-famous locks and canal at Sault Ste. Marie, Michigan are part of the St. Mary's River System.

Corporate headquarters of this owning company are located overlooking the river from the Canadian shoreline opposite the locks complex and power dam control buildings. At the turn of this century. Mr. Francis Hector Clergue planned a massive industrial complex at "The Soo," but failed to see its fulfillment decades later.

The Steamer ALGORIVER is shown below while upbound below Lock One, Welland Ship Canal, on May 11, 1995 with iron ore from Pointe Noire, Quebec for delivery to Acme Steel Company In Chicago. Illinois.

Motor Vessel ALGOSOO (2)

OWNER:	**Algoma Central Marine**
BUILT:	Collingwood Shipyards, Collingwood, Ontario—1974
HULL NO.:	206
O. A. DIMENSIONS:	730′ × 75′ × 44′6″

The modern Motor Vessel ALGOSOO (2) is a self-unloading bulk freighter and is unique in that she was built with her pilot house forward. All other ships built in the period of her design had all cabins aft.

As with the predecessor ship of this name in this fleet, this vessel honors the owning railway with the prefix in the ship name—"ALGO" and the city of the firm's headquarters, Sault Ste. Marie, Ontario, otherwise referred to as the "SOO," in the suffix of the ship name.

Sault Ste. Marie, Ontario is the rail hub of north central Ontario as well as being the home of the largest integrated steel plant in the Dominion of Canada. It also contains the only Canadian lock for interlake navigation on the Upper Lakes.

This ship sailed on its maiden voyage on December 4, 1974 light from Collingwood, Ontario to Badgeley Island, Ontario where it took on 25,935 gross tons of Quartzite Rock for delivery to Midland, Ontario. It is shown above while downbound in the West Neebish Channel, St. Mary's River on August 1, 1982.

Steamer ALGOSOUND

OWNER:	Algoma Central Marine
BUILT:	Canadian Vickers Shipyards, Limited, Montreal, Quebec - 1965
HULL NO.:	285
O.A. DIMENSIONS:	730' x 75' x 39'
FORMER DATA:	Launched as DON-DE-DIEU. Renamed V. W. SCULLY in 1967. Given present name in 1987.

When the bulk freight Steamer ALGOSOUND was first commissioned, it was named for a famous dancing/ballet troupe in Montreal, Quebec in which the original owner, Mr. Phrixos Papachristidis, had a great personal interest.

When it became part of the Labrador Steamship Fleet, it was renamed in honor of an executive at the Steel Company of Canada, and also the Scully Mine in Labrador.

When again renamed in 1987, the familiar ALGO was used along with the first letter, "S," of Mr. Scully's name. A body of water was chosen to provide the name suffix, though no specific body. All sounds that exist in the Great Lakes-St. Lawrence system are the general namesake reference.

The Steamer ALGOSOUND is shown in this photograph passing downbound in the West Neebish Channel, St. Mary's River, on September 2, 1994.

Motor Vessel ALGOSTEEL (2)

OWNER:	Algoma Central Marine
BUILT:	Davie Shipbuilding, Limited, Lauzon, Quebec - 1966
HULL NO.:	658
O. A. DIMENSIONS:	730' x 75' x 39'8"
FORMER DATA:	Launched as the bulk freighter A. S. GLOSSBRENNER. Renamed ALGOGULF in 1987. Converted to a self-unloader at Canadian Shipbuilding & Engineering Limited, St. Catharines, Ontario and given present name in 1990.

The modern self-unloading Motor Vessel ALGOSTEEL (2) sailed on its maiden voyage from Seven Islands, Quebec July 23, 1966 with an iron ore cargo destined for delivery to the "A. & B." Dock at Ashtabula, Ohio.

This carrier established a Great Lakes iron ore cargo record when it took 26,657 gross tons abroad at Port Arthur, Ontario for delivery to Lorain, Ohio in 1967. The record stood until later that season when it was broken by another vessel.

The naming of this vessel on March 31, 1990, by Mrs. Peter Nixon, wife of the president and chief executive officer of Algoma Steel Corporation Limited, signified the long-standing relationship between this owning company and the steel mill at Sault Ste. Marie, Ontario which it has served for over ninety years.

The Motor Vessel ALGOSTEEL (2) is shown in this photograph unloading sand at Port Weller, Ontario, below Lock #1, Welland Ship Canal on May 12, 1990.

Motor Vessel ALGOVILLE

OWNER:	Algoma Central Marine
BUILT:	Saint John Shipbuilding & Dry Dock Company, Limited Saint John, New Brunswick - 1967
HULL NO.:	1084
O. A. DIMENSIONS:	730' x 78' x 39'8"
FORMER DATA:	Launched as SENNEVILLE. Given present name in 1994. Widened midship hull 3' at Port Weller Dry Docks, St. Catharines, Ontario in 1996.

The bulk freight Motor Vessel ALGOVILLE was one of only two such vessels constructed with all deck houses and machinery aft when it and the SILVER ISLE were commissioned in 1967 and 1963, respectively. They were the only two maximum-sized Seaway vessels to have this configuration as gearless bulk freighters.

This carrier sailed on its maiden trip November 8, 1967 with a cargo of iron ore from Sept-Iles, Quebec destined for delivery in Cleveland, Ohio. Managed originally by Mohawk Navigation, then Great Lakes Bulk Carriers, the vessel was actually owned by Pioneer Shipping Limited, a wholly-owned subsidiary of James Richardson & Sons, until its sale to this owner in the spring of 1994. Under its Pioneer Fleet colors, the vessel was "dressed-up" in orange, yellow and white to match the color scheme of Richardson's grain elevators.

When Algoma Central added 7 vessels at one time, some names were chosen simply using their prefix ALGO and the latter part of the vessel's former name, with no specific namesake intended. This was one of those instances. The ship is shown downbound in the West Neebish Channel, St. Mary's River, on July 23, 1998.

Motor Vessel ALGOWAY (2)

OWNER:	Algoma Central Marine
BUILT:	Collingwood Shipyards, Collingwood, Ontario - 1972
HULL NO.:	200
O. A. DIMENSIONS:	650' x 72' x 40'

The self-unloading Motor Vessel ALGOWAY (2) is the second ship in this fleet to bear the name. The first was a small bulk freighter of 6,050 gross tons carrying capacity. It was sold for scrap in 1963 when it became evident that its size and age were sufficient reasons to retire the unit.

The common fleet prefix, ALGO, is used in reference to the first word of the corporate name - Algoma. The suffix, WAY, referred to the Railway which was part of that name when the vessel was constructed.

Today, Algoma Central Corporation continues to have the distinction of being the longest continuously operated fleet of bulk and self-unloaders on the Great Lakes under Canadian flag. In 1999, it celebrated the corporation's 100th anniversary and published an outstanding book of facts and pictures capturing all of the facets of the firm's existence.

The Motor Vessel ALGOWAY (2) is shown above while passing downbound in the West Neebish Channel, St. Mary's River, on June 28, 1982.

Motor Vessel ALGOWEST

OWNER:	Algoma Central Marine
BUILT:	Collingwood Shipyards, Collingwood, Ontario - 1982
HULL NO.:	226
O. A. DIMENSIONS:	730' x 75'10" x 42'
FORMER DATA:	Launched as a bulk freighter. Converted to a self-unloader at Port Weller Dry Docks, St. Catharines, Ontario in 1998.

When this carrier was designed and named, it was for and because a five-year hauling contract existed between Algoma Central and the Canadian Wheat Board. The arrangement called for movement of grain products from Thunder Bay, Ontario through the Great Lakes-Seaway system for delivery to St. Lawrence River ports. It became the first non-self-unloading vessel built new for this fleet since 1968.

The ship sailed on its maiden voyage from Thunder Bay on July 26, 1982 with a cargo of barley destined for delivery to Quebec City, Quebec.

The Canadian Wheat Board is headquartered in Winnipeg, Manitoba and is an agency of the Canadian Government. Its long-range analysis indicated that several more new bulk freighters would be needed to handle expanded export demand. Thus, the agency signed several five-year contracts with Canadian carriers to assist in their financing the new buildings.

The Motor Vessel ALGOWEST is shown upbound in the Welland Ship Canal on May 17, 1999.

Motor Vessel ALGOWOOD

OWNER:	Algoma Central Marine
BUILT:	Collingwood Shipyards, Collingwood, Ontario - 1981
HULL NO.:	219
O. A. DIMENSIONS:	730' x 75'10" x 46'6"

The modern self-unloading Motor Vessel ALGOWOOD was the eleventh new building by Collingwood Shipyards for these owners since their rebuilding of the fleet began in 1964. To honor that long-standing relationship, this name was chosen in specific reference to the town of Collingwood, Ontario. The prefix, *ALGO,* being used again to indicate Algoma Central ownership.

Collingwood, Ontario was first settled by Mr. George Carney in 1835. It was named in honor of Admiral Collingwood, Nelson's second-in-command at Trafalgar. Following siting of a sawmill in 1853 and Canadian National Railways linkage in 1855, the area was granted town status in 1858. Collingwood Shipyards began life early in the 20th century, launching its first ship, Steamer HURONIC, on September 12, 1901.

The Motor Vessel ALGOWOOD was designed with winter navigation in mind, primarily for the run from Marquette, Michigan to Sault Ste. Marie, Ontario with iron ore pellets. It can also trade in the entire Great Lakes - Seaway area. The bow is raked and is a modified ram form to help in late season work. This vessel sailed on its maiden voyage, light from Owen Sound, Ontario to Stoneport, Michigan where it took on a cargo of limestone for Sarnia, Ontario delivery. The departure date was April 6, 1981. The ship is shown while downbound below Lock One, Welland Ship Canal, on April 26, 1988.

Motor Vessel CAPT. HENRY JACKMAN

OWNER:	Algoma Central Marine
BUILT:	Collingwood Shipyards, Collingwood, Ontario - 1981
HULL NO.:	223
O.A. DIMENSIONS:	730' x 75'10" x 42'
FORMER DATA:	Launched as the bulk freighter LAKE WABUSH. Given present name in 1987. Converted to a self-unloader at Canadian Shipbuilding & Engineering Limited, St Catharines, Ontario in 1996.

As a bulk freighter, this vessel sailed on its maiden voyage July 27, 1981 from Thunder Bay, Ontario to Baie Comeau, Quebec with a record cargo of 1,024,383 bushels of wheat. Later in 1981, the ship loaded 1,099,000 bushels of corn to establish another cargo record which still stands.

Captain Henry Jackman was born May 16, 1832 at Goring-on--Sea, Sussex County, England. He received little formal education and migrated to Canada about 1850 with his brother Frank. Henry learned seafaring and took command of Lake Ontario schooners in the 1850-1870 period. The Schooner MARCO POLO, which he commanded, was active in the grain trade. Henry and his brother held ownerships in numerous vessels until 1877 when a series of misfortunes led to financial demise. Capt. Jackman died in Toronto, Ontario on December 2, 1882.

The Motor Vessel CAPT. HENRY JACKMAN is shown inbound at Port Colborne, Ontario, Welland Ship Canal, on April 30, 1997.

Motor Vessel SAUNIÈRE

OWNER:	Algoma Central Marine
BUILT:	Lithgows (1969) Limited East Yard, Port Glasgow, Scotland - 1970
HULL NO.:	1177
O. A. DIMENSIONS:	642'10" x 74'10" x 42'
FORMER DATA:	Launched as the straight deck bulk carrier BROOKNES. Lengthened 122' at Swan, Hunter Shipbuilders, Limited, North Shields, England and renamed ALGOSEA in 1976. Converted to a self-unloader at Herb Fraser and Associates, Port Colborne, Ontario in 1976. Given present name in 1982.

The Motor Vessel SAUNIÈRE took its present name because of a long-term commitment by the owner to move salt from the Magdalen Islands' new salt mine which began operation in 1982. The route of this vessel is westward from the mine area to the province of Quebec ports and other Great Lakes destinations. The ship can, however, traverse any of the oceans of the world as well.

The capability of this fleet to serve both Great Lakes waters and the oceans of the world is not new, but stems from over eighty years ago when chartered ships first ran between Sault Ste. Marie, Ontario and England for this line.

The namesake of this vessel is the French word on the bow which means, literally, "salt box." The ship is shown while downbound in the Welland Ship Canal with a cargo of salt on November 24, 1982.

Motor Vessel ALGOCATALYST

OWNER:	Algoma Tankers Limited
BUILT:	Robb Caledon Shipbuilding Limited, Dundee, Scotland - 1972
HULL NO.:	557
O.A. DIMENSIONS:	431' x 62'4" x 34'5"
FORMER DATA:	Launched as JON RAMSØY Renamed DOAN TRANSPORT in 1974. Renamed ENERCHEM CATALYST in 1986. Given present name 1999.

The tank Motor Vessel ALGOCATALYST was one of three Enerchem vessels acquired by this owner early in 1999. The other two were not put into service, nor renamed, because it was judged that this was the only carrier of the three worth operating. That is because it was the only tanker with a double hull. Double hull tankers are being mandated because of pollution concerns.

When renamed, this vessel added the familiar ALGO prefix and kept CATALYST. This word may be defined as "substance (or carrier thereof) that initiates a chemical reaction and enables it to proceed under milder conditions than otherwise possible."

The ALGOCATALYST is shown below Lock 7, downbound in the Welland Ship Canal, destined for Mississauga, Ontario on April 3, 2000.

Motor Vessel ALGOEAST

OWNER:	Algoma Tankers Limited
BUILT:	Mitsubishi Heavy Industries Limited, Shimonoseki, Japan - 1977
HULL NO.:	779
O. A. DIMENSIONS:	431'5" x 65'7" x 35'5"
FORMER DATA:	Launched as TEXACO BRAVE (2). Renamed LE BRAVE in 1986. Renamed IMPERIAL ST. LAWRENCE (2) in 1997. Given present name in 1998.

The tank Motor Vessel ALGOEAST was built outside the British Commonwealth at a time when all shipyards in Canada were fully booked. At the time, it was the only way for Texaco Canada to obtain badly needed new tonnage for their movement of petroleum products on the Great Lakes-St. Lawrence Seaway system. A waiver from the government was granted to permit this foreign building.

When Texaco left the marine hauling business it chartered its vessels to Socanav. Then, all of Texaco Canada was bought by Imperial Oil Limited in the early 1990's. With Imperial's decision to divest itself of the majority of its marine fleet on the east coast in 1997 and culmination of the sale to this owner in January 1998, this ship passed into this ownership.

The namesake reference is to the eastern operations of Imperial Oil. The tanker is shown in this photograph upbound below Lock 1 in the Welland Ship Canal on September 15, 1998.

Motor Vessel ALGOFAX

OWNER:	Algoma Tankers Limited
BUILT:	Davie Shipbuilding, Limited, Lauzon, Quebec - 1969
HULL NO.:	666
O. A. DIMENSIONS:	485'5" x 70'2" x 33'3"
FORMER DATA:	Launched as IMPERIAL BEDFORD. Given present name in 1998.

The large refinery operations of Imperial Oil on the east coast of Canada are located at Dartmouth, Nova Scotia. It is a site not far distant from the much larger community of Halifax.

It seemed appropriate to managers of Algoma Central Corporation to rename this carrier in honor of Halifax and its surrounding area when the ship was acquired in early 1998. Halifax is the capital of Nova Scotia and a major seaport of Canada. It is located on a peninsula and an inlet of the Atlantic Ocean. It was founded in 1749 as a British naval base intended to rival the French port of Louisburg. The port is open year-around to waterborne traffic.

This tanker was the first to bring crude oil from the Canadian High Arctic into Montreal, Quebec harbor when she arrived in that port on September 10, 1985. The cargo was loaded from another ship at Little Cornwallis Island, just 60 kilometers from the magnetic North Pole.

The Motor Vessel ALGOFAX is shown upbound in the Welland Ship Canal on May 27, 1998.

Motor Vessel ALGONOVA

OWNER:	Algoma Tankers Limited
BUILT:	Collingwood Shipyards, Collingwood, Ontario - 1969
HULL NO.:	193
O. A. DIMENSIONS:	400'6" x 54'2" x 26'5"
FORMER DATA:	Launched as TEXACO CHIEF (2). Renamed A. G. FARQUHARSON in 1986. Given present name in 1998.

This petroleum tanker takes its name from the province of NOVA Scotia in the Maritime region of Canada.

Although not included in the original purchase of the Imperial Oil Fleet by Algoma Tankers Limited, the carrier was of little use to Imperial as a "one boat" Great Lakes fleet. Following additional negotiations between the parties, this vessel was also purchased by Algoma in March 1998. Besides being a back-up vessel, its addition to this fleet provided an opportunity to expand liquid cargo carriage beyond the precise needs of Imperial Oil.

The Motor Vessel ALGONOVA has a carrying capacity of 8,422 cubic meters in its fifteen cargo tanks when loaded to its mid-summer draft.

The tanker is shown in this photograph upbound in Lake Nicolet, St. Mary's River, with fuel oil bound for Thunder Bay, Ontario on July 22, 1998.

Motor Vessel ALGOSAR

OWNER:	Algoma Tankers Limited
BUILT:	Port Weller Dry Docks Limited, St. Catharines, Ontario - 1974
HULL NO.:	57
O. A. DIMENSIONS:	435' x 74' x 32'
FORMER DATA:	Launched as IMPERIAL ST. CLAIR. Given present name in 1998.

The 106,000 barrel capacity tank Motor Vessel ALGOSAR utilizes the familiar ALGO as the ship name prefix and specifically honors the Imperial Oil refinery operations at Sarnia, Ontario as its namesake.

Sarnia lies opposite Port Huron, Michigan at the head of the St. Clair River. That river connects Lake St. Clair with Lake Huron and is a vital link for Great Lakes and international commerce.

The city of Sarnia has been termed the "Heart of Canada's Chemical Valley" because it contains one of the country's largest oil refineries, largest Fiberglass plant and only synthetic-rubber plant. All of these facilities utilize water-borne Great Lakes commerce in their operations.

The Motor Vessel ALGOSAR is shown in this photograph approaching Lock 8 at the southern end of the Welland Ship Canal on August 24, 1998. It is loaded with fuel oil from Nanticoke, Ontario bound for lower St. Lawrence River delivery.

Motor Vessel ALGOSCOTIA

OWNER:	Algoma Tankers Limited
BUILT:	Port Weller Dry Docks Limited, St. Catharines, Ontario - 1966
HULL NO.:	39
O. A. DIMENSIONS:	440' x 60' x 31'
FORMER DATA:	Launched as IMPERIAL ACADIA. Given present name in 1998.

The petroleum product tank Motor Vessel ALGOSCOTIA takes its name with reference to the Canadian province of Nova Scotia and utilizes the fleet theme prefix of ALGO in the name.

The old French name for the province is Acadie and was given in the days of the first settlements by the French in the Atlantic seaboard possessions of the New World. Origin of the name in English is not precisely known, but is believed to be Indian in reference to early tribes which inhabited the area.

This carrier was part of a four-vessel acquisition by the Algoma Central Corporation's wholly-owned subsidiary noted above in early 1998. It continues to haul petroleum products for Imperial, primarily from and to its large refinery at Dartmouth, Nova Scotia which is not far distant from Halifax.

The Motor Vessel ALGOSCOTIA is shown in this photograph in Halifax, Nova Scotia harbor on September 23, 1998.

Motor Vessel AMERICAN MARINER

OWNER:	American Steamship Company
BUILT:	Bay Shipbuilding Corporation, Sturgeon Bay, Wisconsin - 1980
HULL NO.:	723
O. A. DIMENSIONS:	730′ x 78′ x 45′

The self-unloading Motor Vessel AMERICAN MARINER was to have been named CHICAGO (3) in honor of the headquarters city of the parent company, General American Transportation Corporation (GATX). After the name was painted on the hull, however, and before it was documented, the decision was made to give the new vessel this name.

The first word of the ship name honors the name of the steamship company, a subsidiary of GATX. The second word is the specific namesake reference and relates to the seamen who actually operate the vessels in this self-unloader fleet. The word mariner is defined as "one who navigates or assists in navigating a ship." Synonyms of the word mariner are seaman or sailor.

The Motor Vessel AMERICAN MARINER sailed on its maiden voyage, light from Sturgeon Bay, Wisconsin to Escanaba, Michigan to load iron ore pellets destined for Ashtabula, Ohio on April 26, 1980. It is shown while downbound in the West Neebish Channel, St. Mary's River, on July 16, 1990.

Motor Vessel AMERICAN REPUBLIC

OWNER: American Steamship Company
BUILT: Bay Shipbuilding Corporation, Sturgeon Bay, Wisconsin - 1981
HULL NO.: 724
O. A. DIMENSIONS: 634'10" x 68' x 40'

The self-unloading bulk freight Motor Vessel AMERICAN REPUBLIC is a one-of-a-kind ship on the Great Lakes that was specially designed and constructed to be the main shuttle ship for the transportation of iron ore pellets between the Lorain Pellet Terminal of then Republic Steel Corporation at Lorain, Ohio and their upriver steel mills at the head of navigation on the Cuyahoga River in Cleveland, Ohio. While capable of longer open lake runs, its main purpose is to service the above trade route. In a year of normal steel demand, the vessel makes about 175 round trips.

The special design features include kort nozzels on the stern, a series of flanking rudders and an all-window pilothouse. The latter is for backing the ship out of the Cuyahoga River because it is too large to wind.

The namesakes of the ship are the *AMERICAN* Steamship Company, owners, and *REPUBLIC* Steel Corporation, long-term users of the vessel under a floating contract. Republic recently became integrated into LTV Steel Company.

This vessel sailed on its maiden trip May 21, 1981, light from Sturgeon Bay, Wisconsin to Escanaba, Michigan, to load iron ore pellets for Cleveland, Ohio delivery. It is shown in the Cuyahoga River, inbound at Cleveland, Ohio with a cargo of limestone on October 2, 1982.

Motor Vessel JOHN J. BOLAND (4)

OWNER:	American Steamship Company
BUILT:	Bay Shipbuilding Corporation, Sturgeon Bay, Wisconsin - 1973
HULL NO.:	710
O.A. DIMENSIONS:	680' x 78' x 45'
FORMER DATA:	Launched as CHARLES E. WILSON. Given present name in 2000.

Mr. John James Boland was the recognized patriarch of Great Lakes shipping. He was born in Buffalo, New York on September 20, 1875 and began his prominent career in Great Lakes shipping in 1895 by organizing a vessel brokerage business in Buffalo, New York. In 1902 he purchased the Steamer YALE, the first steel ship owned by any Buffalo company other than the railroads. In 1904 he formed a partnership with Mr. Adam E. Cornelius becoming the firm of Boland & Cornelius, of which Mr. Boland was president. An outgrowth of this was the 1907 formation of American Steamship Company.

Mr. Boland died unexpectedly on October 3, 1956. He was a man of genial and engaging personality and had been selected as the Great Lakes Man of the Year on May 19, 1956.

His namesake sailed on its maiden trip September 20, 1973 in ballast from Sturgeon Bay, Wisconsin to Escanaba, Michigan to load iron ore pellets. It is shown in this photograph just after being renamed in March 2000 at Superior, Wisconsin.

Motor Vessel BUFFALO (3)

OWNER:	American Steamship Company
BUILT:	Bay Shipbuilding Corporation, Sturgeon Bay, Wisconsin - 1978
HULL NO.:	721
O. A. DIMENSIONS:	634'10" x 68' x 40'

The namesake of this vessel is the operating headquarters of the fleet – Buffalo, New York, sometimes known as the "Queen City of the Lakes." Buffalo is located at the eastern end of Lake Erie and is the heart of what remains of the milling industry fed by Great Lakes grain-carrying ships. It is the seat of Erie County and was the site, in 1679, of the building of La Salle's bark LE GRIFFON. This was the first vessel larger than a canoe to sail on the Upper Great Lakes. The city was also the port of hail of the famous WALK-IN-THE-WATER, first steamship to run on the Upper Great Lakes. The city was settled in 1790, was plotted in 1803 and was incorporated as a village in 1816. It was given status as a city in 1832.

The Motor Vessel BUFFALO (3) sailed on its maiden trip light from Sturgeon Bay, Wisconsin on September 23, 1978 to Escanaba, Michigan where it loaded 20,910 gross tons of iron ore for Indiana Harbor, Indiana delivery. It is shown in the photograph while downbound with iron ore in the West Neebish Channel, St. Mary's River on August 9, 1981.

Motor Vessel ADAM E. CORNELIUS (4)

OWNER:	American Steamship Company
BUILT:	American Ship Building Company, Toledo, Ohio - 1973
HULL NO.:	200
O. A. DIMENSIONS:	680' x 78' x 42'
FORMER DATA:	Launched as ROGER M. KYES. Given present name in 1989.

The self-unloading bulk freight Motor Vessel ADAM E. CORNELIUS (4) sailed on its maiden trip August 22, 1973, light from Toledo, Ohio to Escanaba, Michigan to load iron ore pellets.

Mr. Adam Edward Cornelius was half of the original two-family father and son team of vessel operators and brokers, which was unique on the Lakes. He was born June 25, 1882 in Buffalo, New York. After high school graduation, he began working as a clerk and stenographer in a vessel brokerage office in 1901. In 1904, he and Mr. John J. Boland became partners in Boland and Cornelius. Their purchase of ships began in 1907. This was the start of the American Steamship Company. Mr. Cornelius became chairman of the board of the firm in 1915 and remained in that post until his death in Buffalo, New York on December 10, 1953.

Mr. Cornelius' fourth namesake vessel was named in honor of his remembrance by his daughter-in-law, at Buffalo, New York on June 15, 1989. It is shown in this photograph while upbound in the Middle Neebish Channel, St. Mary's River, loaded with 21,718 net tons of salt on July 24, 1989.

Motor Vessel INDIANA HARBOR

OWNER:	American Steamship Company
BUILT:	Bay Shipbuilding Corporation, Sturgeon Bay, Wisconsin - 1979
HULL NO.:	719
O. A. DIMENSIONS:	1,000′ x 105′ x 56′

The modern self-unloading Motor Vessel INDIANA HARBOR takes its name in reference to the port complex at East Chicago, Indiana where Inland Steel Company and another large steel plant receive huge quantities of raw materials via the Great Lakes. This vessel began service to Inland in 1979 and honored that business relationship in this name.

Inland Steel Company produces all of its raw steel at its Indiana Harbor Works. The site occupies approximately 1,700 acres for coke ovens, blast furnaces, open hearths, basic oxygen furnaces and electric furnaces. 99% of the products are carbon and high-strength, low-alloy steel.

East Chicago, Indiana was laid out in 1887 and was incorporated in 1889. It is about twenty miles southeast of downtown Chicago and is a heavily industrialized city. Not only the steel plants, but oil refineries and associated heavy industry abounds in the vicinity.

The Motor Vessel INDIANA HARBOR was christened on July 11, 1979 and sailed on its maiden voyage on August 29, 1979, light from Sturgeon Bay, Wisconsin for Two Harbors, Minnesota to load iron ore pellets for its namesake port's delivery. It is shown above barely 24 hours old, in the Middle Neebish Channel, St. Mary's River, on that maiden trip, on August 30, 1979.

Motor Vessel SAM LAUD

OWNER:	American Steamship Company
BUILT:	Bay Shipbuilding Corporation, Sturgeon Bay, Wisconsin - 1975
HULL NO.:	712
O. A. DIMENSIONS:	634'10" x 68' x 40'

The self-unloading Motor Vessel SAM LAUD is named in honor of a life-long employee and executive of this fleet's parent company. Mr. Sam Laud was born in Brooklyn, New York, November 17, 1896 and was educated in the public schools. He began working as a trainee and riveter for General American Transportation Corporation in East Chicago, Indiana in 1916. After service in France in World War I, Mr. Laud rejoined General American and was named assistant controller in 1923, being further advanced to general manager of the tank car manufacturing division at Masury, Ohio in 1927.

In 1930 he was promoted to executive assistant to the president and was elected a director in 1934. In 1945 Mr. Laud became president of the firm. He was elected vice chairman in 1954 and chairman of the board in 1956. In 1960 Mr. Laud took over as chairman of the executive committee while his successor was being groomed. He died at Chicago, Illinois on August 1, 1963. Until his death he was a director of many concerns including the First National Bank of East Chicago, Jewish Federation of Metropolitan Chicago and Michael Reese Research Foundation.

This vessel sailed on its maiden voyage April 29, 1975 light from Sturgeon Bay, Wisconsin for Escanaba, Michigan to load iron ore pellets for Indiana Harbor, Indiana. It is shown above while taking on a cargo of coal at South Chicago, Illinois on November 26, 1979.

Motor Vessel WALTER J. McCARTHY, JR.

OWNER:	American Steamship Company
BUILT:	Bay Shipbuilding Corporation, Sturgeon Bay, Wisconsin - 1977
HULL NO.:	716
O. A. DIMENSIONS:	1,000' x 105' x 56'
FORMER DATA:	Launched as BELLE RIVER. Given present name in 1990.

The Motor Vessel WALTER J. McCARTHY, JR. was specifically designed as a collier, that is, it was built for high cubic measurements in its holds to accommodate the coal cargoes originating at Superior, Wisconsin and destined for St. Clair, Michigan delivery, to power plants of the Detroit Edison Company.

The ship sailed on its maiden voyage, light from Sturgeon Bay, to Superior, Wisconsin on August 31, 1977 where it departed on September 3rd with a new Great Lakes coal cargo record - 62,802 net tons. The carrier is shown passing downbound in the West Neebish Channel, St. Mary's River, on June 10, 1990.

Namesake of this vessel is Mr. Walter John McCarthy, Jr. who was born in New York, New York on April 20, 1925. He earned a B.S. degree in mechanical engineering from Cornell University in 1949 and worked as an engineer with the Public Service Electric & Gas Company until 1956. He then became section head of the Atomic Power Development Association in Detroit, Michigan and left that post in 1961 to become general manager of the Power Reactor Development Company. He joined Detroit Edison in 1968 as executive vice president-operations, was named president in 1979 and chairman of the board and chief executive in 1981. He retired May 1, 1990. Mr. McCarthy is an avid Great Lakes shipping fan and boat-watcher.

Motor Vessel ST. CLAIR (2)

OWNER:	American Steamship Company
BUILT:	Bay Shipbuilding Corporation, Sturgeon Bay, Wisconsin - 1976
HULL NO.:	714
O. A. DIMENSIONS:	770′ x 92′ x 52′

The Motor Vessel ST. CLAIR (2) departed Sturgeon Bay, Wisconsin May 4, 1976 on its maiden voyage and loaded iron ore at Escanaba, Michigan for Indiana Harbor, Indiana delivery the following day. It became the largest vessel ever to be side-launched when dropped into the water in January, 1976. The ship was built as an interim step towards the following vessel, a 1,000-footer, ready in 1977. The primary purpose of this unit of the fleet is to move coal from Superior, Wisconsin to St. Clair, Michigan.

Namesake of this vessel is the St. Clair power plant of the Detroit Edison Company, located on the St. Clair River at St. Clair, Michigan. At the time of the vessel's initial sailing, the plant had a generating capacity of 1.8 million kilowatts, enough to supply power to about two million people in the service area. This plant is the first to use large quantities of low-sulphur Western coal shipped by Great Lakes carriers.

While the specific namesake of this ship is the power plant named above, the whole area and river took its name from the fact that La Salle, an early Great Lakes navigator and explorer, first entered the lower areas of the river on the Feast of Santa Clara, August 12, 1679. He named the river in honor of that event.

The vessel is shown above while downbound with coal in Whitefish Bay, Lake Superior, on October 24, 1986.

Motor Vessel H. LEE WHITE (2)

OWNER: American Steamship Company
BUILT: Bay Shipbuilding Corporation, Sturgeon Bay, Wisconsin—1974
HULL NO.: 711
O. A. DIMENSIONS: 704′ × 78′ × 45′

The namesake of this self-unloader is Mr. Harris Lee White, late chairman of the board of this owning company. Mr. White was born in Oswego, New York on August 13, 1912 and received a B.A. degree from Hamilton College in 1934. In 1937 he was awarded an Ll.B. degree from Cornell University and was admitted to the New York Bar the same year.

He was special assistant to the general counsel at U.S. Casualty Company in 1937 and was on the staff of Pearis & Resseguie in 1938. From 1939 to 1943, Mr. White was associated with Mangan & Mangan and after World War II joined Cadwalader, Wickersham & Taft in 1946, becoming a partner in the firm in 1949.

Mr. White became interested in ships during these years and through his own and others' efforts became a leading ship owner and manager with over 100 vessels in various fleets on the oceans and Great Lakes. Mr. White died suddenly in New York City on September 27, 1969. His namesake sailed on its maiden voyage June 1, 1974, light from Sturgeon Bay, Wisconsin to Escanaba, Michigan to load iron ore pellets for delivery to Indiana Harbor, Indiana. It is shown unloading limestone at Huron, Ohio on September 10, 1981.

Motor Vessel BURNS HARBOR

OWNER:	Bethlehem Steel Corporation, Great Lakes Steamship Division
BUILT:	Bay Shipbuilding Corporation, Sturgeon Bay, Wisconsin - 1980
HULL NO.:	720
O. A. DIMENSIONS:	1,000′ x 105′ x 56′

The modern self-unloading Motor Vessel BURNS HARBOR is named for this firm's newest fully-integrated steelmaking complex located at Burns Harbor, Indiana about 30 miles southeast of Chicago, Illinois. It was because of the growth of this facility, originally begun in 1962, that this vessel was built to bring in iron ore pellets from Lake Superior. The plant's first cargo of iron ore was delivered on September 11, 1969 by the Steamer LEHIGH. This nation's largest blast furnaces, an 82-oven coke battery and over 80 other related buildings comprise this efficient plant today.

The plant got its name because Burn's Ditch flows into Lake Michigan at the site. Mr. Randall W. Burns, owner of 1,200 acres in the area, petitioned Porter County to provide drainage of the marshy land so that it could be put to useful purpose under cultivation.

The Motor Vessel BURNS HARBOR is shown upbound above the Soo Locks on August 17, 1985. The ship sailed on its maiden voyage, light from Sturgeon Bay, Wisconsin on September 28, 1980, to Superior, Wisconsin to load iron ore pellets.

Motor Vessel STEWART J. CORT

OWNER:	Bethlehem Steel Corporation, Great Lakes Steamship Division
BUILT:	Bow & Stern: Ingalls Shipbuilding Corporation, Pascagoula, Mississippi—1970; Midbody: Erie Marine, Erie, Pennsylvania—1971.
HULL NO.:	1173 (Ingalls) & 101 (Erie)
O. A. DIMENSIONS:	1,000′ × 105′ × 49′

The Motor Vessel STEWART J. CORT sailed on its maiden voyage from Erie, Pennsylvania on May 1, 1972 and headed light for Taconite Harbor, Minnesota where it took on 49,343 gross tons of iron ore pellets for Burns Harbor, Indiana delivery, thus establishing a new all-time Great Lakes cargo record for any vessel in any commodity. It is shown above downbound in Sault Ste. Marie Harbor on July 3, 1978.

Mr. Stewart Joseph Cort was this ship's namesake. He was born in Rochelle, Illinois on March 16, 1881 and graduated from Lehigh University with an M.E. degree in 1906 at which time he joined the Duquesne Works of Carnegie Steel Company. In 1909 he became assistant superintendent of the Cambria plant of Midvale Steel & Ordinance Company, and, in 1916 he was named superintendent.

In 1917 he joined Bethlehem Steel Company at the Saucon Works in Bethlehem, Pennsylvania as superintendent. He became general manager of the Sparrows Point plant in 1928 and was elected vice president of all steel operations at Bethlehem in 1947. He served in this capacity and as a director until retiring in 1957. Mr. Cort died at Bethlehem, Pennsylvania on September 23, 1958.

Motor Vessel JOS. F. BIGANE

OWNER: Bigane Vessel Fueling Company of Chicago
BUILT: Halter Marine Services, Incorporated, New Orleans, Louisiana - 1973
HULL NO.: 368
O. A. DIMENSIONS: 130' x 40' x 14'

The 7,500 barrel capacity tank Motor Vessel JOS. F. BIGANE is named in honor of Mr. Joseph Francis Bigane who was born in Chicago, Illinois on April 22, 1893. He received his education in parochial schools and graduated from St. Ignatius High School in 1911 at which time he began working in the firm of John Bigane & Sons Coal Company. This company was a partnership between his father and brother in Chicago, Illinois.

In due course Mr. Bigane assumed wider roles in management of the business and became chief executive on the death of his father in 1932.

In 1953 the partnership was incorporated and separate firms set up to give their business affairs separate identity types. Mr. Bigane then became chairman of the board of Bigane Coal Company, Bigane Oil Company and Bigane Paving Company. He retains that post in these firms at this time. His son, Joseph F. Bigane, Jr. is president of this vessel-owning firm and serves as secretary of the above named firms.

This modern fueling vessel pays tribute to a successful man and his family's ongoing enterprises. It is shown in the photo above while on trial runs in the spring of 1973 in the Gulf of Mexico.

Barge ST. MARYS CEMENT

OWNER:	Blue Circle Cement Company
BUILT:	The Toledo Shipyard, Toledo, Ohio - 1986
HULL NO.:	8601
O. A. DIMENSIONS:	360' x 60' x 23'3"

The Barge ST. MARYS CEMENT was specifically designed for the carriage of finished bulk cement from the Detroit, Michigan plant of this owning company to its various distribution terminals around the Great Lakes. It was also the first hull built at Toledo, Ohio on the site of the former Amercian Ship Building Company which had ceased operating there several years previously.

This cement-carrying barge was christened May 24, 1986 and has a carrying capacity of 9,400 net tons at a summer loadline of 19'8".

Namesake of this carrier is the St. Mary's Cement Company itself. It was formed in 1912 by the Lind and Rogers families of St. Marys, Ontario. St. Marys was sold to this firm in 1998.

The original cement plant was located in St. Marys and was expanded in 1975. A plant at Bowmanville, Ontario, on Lake Ontario, was opened in 1968. The former Peerless Cement plant on the Rouge River in Detroit, Michigan was acquired in 1983, to service distribution terminals in Wisconsin and Illinois. This barge was built to provide Great Lakes transport to those U.S. destinations. It is shown while inbound on its maiden voyage from Toledo, Ohio to the St. Marys cement dock on the Rouge River, Detroit, Michigan on June 29, 1986.

Barge ST. MARYS CEMENT II

OWNER:	Blue Circle Cement Company
BUILT:	Galveston Shipbuilding Company, Galveston, Texas - 1978
HULL NO.:	121
O. A. DIMENSIONS:	469'6" x 76' x 35'
FORMER DATA:	Launched as the tank barge VELASCO. Renamed CANMAR SHUTTLE in 1981. Given present name in 1990. Converted to a self-unloading dry bulk cargo barge at E. S. Fox Limited, Welland, Ontario in 1992.

This barge was the second unit in the combined Canadian and United States fleets of St. Marys Cement Company, thus the use of the "II" designation. The namesake reference was specifically to the owning company.

Bowmanville, Ontario is the site of a large cement manufacturing plant of St. Marys. As shipping requirements grew, the firm decided to acquire this second vessel to carry its production from Bowmanville to various other ports in Canada and the United States at which it had distribution terminals.

Rather than being able to handle only cement, this vessel has a boom which can deliver material to piles ashore for open storage of such products as clinker, coal and other such commodities.

The Barge ST. MARYS CEMENT II is shown five hours into its maiden trip, downbound below Lock # 4 of the Welland Ship Canal, on September 11, 1992. The vessel was enroute to Bowmanville, Ontario to load cement clinker for delivery to Detroit, Michigan.

Barge ST. MARYS CEMENT III

OWNER:	Blue Circle Cement Company
BUILT:	Robin Shipyard (PTE) Ltd., Singapore, Singapore - 1980
HULL NO.:	310
O. A. DIMENSIONS:	335' x 76'8" x 17'9"
FORMER DATA:	Launched as BIGORANGE XVI. Renamed SAYS in 1985. Renamed AL-SAYB-7 in 1985. Renamed CLARKSON CARRIER in 1986. Given present name in 1994.

This owning company acquired this bulk cement-carrying barge from the St. Lawrence Cement Company, its prior owner, in the spring of 1994. At that time, the barge had a carrying capacity of only 4,800 gross tons. Plans were immediately set for enlarging this capacity during the winter of 1994-95 so that current capacity is 7,200 gross tons.

No major external work was required to accomplish this increase, but extensive scantling additions to allow a deeper loadline was. To an observer, therefore, except for being now "dressed" in St. Marys' colors, the vessel appears the same.

The Tug PETITE FORTE was retained under long-term charter to provide motive power for the barge. The namesake reference is to the fact that this was the third unit in St. Marys' fleet when they acquired it. The tug and barge are shown above at St. Marys' terminal in Cleveland, Ohio on May 3, 1995 shortly after having arrived from Bowmanville, Ontario with a cargo of finished cement.

Motor Vessel ATLANTIC ERIE

OWNER:	Canada Steamship Lines, Inc.
BUILT:	Collingwood Shipyards, Collingwood, Ontario - 1985
HULL NO.:	225
O. A. DIMENSIONS:	736'6" x 75'10" x 50'
FORMER DATA:	Launched as HON. PAUL MARTIN. Given present name in 1988.

Although similar in appearance to many other modern self-unloading bulk vessels, the Motor Vessel ATLANTIC ERIE was the largest vessel ever built and launched at Collingwood when that event occurred on November 1, 1984. Following some use on the Great Lakes during 1985-1988, the carrier was given this name for the majority of its operation on the high seas.

The vessel then began dual ocean and Great Lakes service during late 1998. The name signifys this service, ATLANTIC being in reference to the Atlantic Ocean and ERIE referring to Lake Erie.

The Motor Vessel ATLANTIC ERIE sailed on its maiden voyage April 19, 1985 with a cargo of grain from Thunder Bay, Ontario to Quebec City, Quebec. The self-unloader is shown in this photograph while downbound in the West Neebish Channel, St. Mary's River, on September 19, 1999.

Motor Vessel ATLANTIC HURON

OWNER:	Canada Steamship Lines, Inc.
BUILT:	Collingwood Shipyards, Collingwood, Ontario - 1984
HULL NO.:	227
O.A. DIMENSIONS:	736'6" x 75'10" x 46'6"
FORMER DATA:	Launched as the bulk freighter PRAIRIE HARVEST. Converted to a self-unloader at Port Weller Dry Docks, St. Catharines, Ontario and renamed ATLANTIC HURON in 1989. Renamed MELVIN H. BAKER II in 1994. Renamed ATLANTIC HURON, for the second time, in 1997.

When this ship was designed and built, the plan for future conversion to a self-unloader was in the minds of the owners. They carried out that plan during the 1989 season. The carrier was laid-up at the end of 1988, then the work was performed so that the ship sailed December 1st under its new configuration.

A unique feature was built into the vessel in 1984 which permitted a bow design that was innovative. The design of the bow permits the underwater extended ram portion to be inserted beneath the lowered lock boom at exits of Seaway locks. This had the effect of allowing the ship's overall length to be 6'6" greater than any carrier built for the system to that date.

The Motor Vessel ATLANTIC HURON sailed on its maiden trip April 6, 1984 from Collingwood, Ontario to Thunder Bay, Ontario to load a cargo of wheat destined for Port Cartier, Quebec delivery. The vessel is shown while underway in the Welland Ship Canal between Locks 3 and 4 on July 10, 1998.

Motor Vessel M. H. BAKER III

OWNER:	Canada Steamship Lines, Inc.
BUILT:	Collingwood Shipyards, Collingwood, Ontario - 1982
HULL NO.:	222
O. A. DIMENSIONS:	736' x 75'10" x 50'
FORMER DATA:	Launched as ATLANTIC SUPERIOR. Renamed M. H. BAKER III in 1997.

This vessel was renamed in 1997 in honor of the late Melvin Houston Baker because the ship was engaged in transport of cargoes for the National Gypsum Company on a long-term contract.

Mr. Baker was born August 11, 1885 in Sevierville, Tennessee and attended Carson-Newman College. He began working as a salesman for several firms before becoming secretary and general manager of National Gypsum upon its incorporation on August 29, 1925. He was elected president of the firm in 1928 and chairman of the board in 1952, serving in that capacity until December 31, 1964. Mr. Baker was then named honorary chairman and held that title when he died on June 25, 1972.

The Motor Vessel M. H. BAKER III sailed on its maiden trip June 25, 1982, in ballast from Thunder Bay, Ontario to Superior, Wisconsin to load iron ore pellets for Sault Ste. Marie, Ontario. The carrier is shown in this photograph while unloading a cargo of gypsum in September 1997 at Portsmouth, New Hampshire.

Motor Vessel CSL NIAGARA

OWNER:	Canada Steamship Lines, Inc.
BUILT:	Collingwood Shipyards, Collingwood, Ontario - 1972
HULL NO.:	197
O. A. DIMENSIONS:	740' x 78' x 48'5"
FORMER DATA:	Launched as J. W. McGIFFIN. Lengthened 10', widened 3', deepened 1'11" and given present name in 1999 at Port Weller Dry Docks, St. Catherines, Ontario.

Christened on June 15, 1999, this self-unloader was the first in a rebuilding program to see this enlargement. That came about because of new St. Lawrence Seaway regulations which allowed this size vessel to traverse the system. Canada Steamship Lines committed to three such enlargements, and had options on two more as of this writing.

The enlargement was done by severing the forebody forward of the stern and building an all-new midbody, but salvaging most of the self-unloading gear that was still quite serviceable.

A new name was chosen since the work done at Port Weller was termed Hull 77 while underway, and the former namesake had died. Besides the first 3 letters noting the owner's name, the specific namesake was the Niagara Peninsula and Niagara Frontier which have been prominent in the development of Great Lakes shipping.

The Motor Vessel CSL NIAGARA is shown above on July 30, 1999 at Port Colborne, Ontario with its first cargo, 35,655 net tons of coal, from Sandusky, Ohio destined for Hamilton, Ontario delivery.

Motor Vessel LOUIS R. DESMARAIS

OWNER:	Canada Steamship Lines, Inc.
BUILT:	Collingwood Shipyards, Collingwood, Ontario - 1977
HULL NO.:	212
O.A. DIMENSIONS:	730' x 75' x 46'6"

Mr. Louis Roger Desmarais was born in Sudbury, Ontario on February 16, 1923. He received a B.S. degree from McGill University in 1945 and also became a chartered accountant the same year. He joined Courtois, Fredette & Co., in 1945, but formed Desmarais, Parisien in 1951 at Sudbury. After returning to Montreal, Quebec in 1965, he worked for various firms until being elected president of Canada Steamship Lines in 1968.

He was the steamship line's chairman of the board from 1973 until 1977 when he resigned to become chairman of the Council for Canadian Unity. He has continued active in various civic and corporate affairs.

His namesake sailed on its maiden trip light from Owen Sound, Ontario November 3, 1977 for Thunder Bay, Ontario where it loaded 27,117 gross tons of iron ore pellets for delivery to Hamilton, Ontario.

The Motor Vessel LOUIS R. DESMARAIS is shown in this photograph while downbound in the West Neebish Channel, St.Mary's River, on September 1, 1997.

Motor Vessel FRONTENAC (5)

OWNER:	Canada Steamship Lines Inc.
BUILT:	Davie Shipbuilding, Limited, Lauzon, Quebec—1968
HULL NO.:	661
O. A. DIMENSIONS:	729′7″ × 75′3″ × 39′8″
FORMER DATA:	Launched as a bulk freighter. Converted to a self-unloader at Collingwood Shipyards, Collingwood, Ontario in 1973.

This vessel is named in honor of Mr. Louis de Buade, Comte de Frontenac et Palluau who was governor of New France from 1672 to 1682 and from 1689 to 1698. He was born at Ste. Germain-en Laye, France in 1620. His office of governor of New France came by appointment in France and he was given authority to preside over French possessions in North America.

Frontenac established municipal government in Quebec but was recalled in 1682 because of divided factions there. He was restored to power in 1689 and held the post until his death in Quebec City in 1698. He was known for his tactful dealings with Indians and encouragement of French exploration into the west.

The self-unloading Motor Vessel FRONTENAC (5) is shown while she is down-bound on Lake St. Clair with a cargo of iron ore for Hamilton, Ontario on October 5, 1980.

Steamer HALIFAX

OWNER: Canada Steamship Lines, Inc.
BUILT: Davie Shipbuilding, Limited, Lauzon, Quebec - 1963
HULL NO.: 638
O. A. DIMENSIONS: 730' x 75' x 39'3"
FORMER DATA: Launched as the bulk freighter FRANKCLIFFE HALL (2). Converted to a self-unloader and deepened 6' at Port Arthur Shipbuilding Company, Thunder Bay, Ontario in 1980. Given present name in 1988.

The Steamer HALIFAX sailed on its maiden voyage light from Luzon, Quebec to Duluth, Minnesota to load an export cargo of grain on May 29, 1963.

Its namesake is the capital of the province of Nova Scotia. Halifax is a major seaport of Canada and is located on a peninsula which extends into Halifax Harbor, an inlet of the Atlantic Ocean. It is about 200 miles southwest of Sydney, Nova Scotia. It was founded in 1749 as a British naval base intended to rival the French port of Louisburg.

The Steamer HALIFAX is shown in this photograph passing downbound in the West Neebish Channel, St. Mary's River, on June 6, 1998.

Motor Vessel MANITOULIN (5)

OWNER:	Canada Steamship Lines, Inc.
BUILT:	Davie Shipbuilding, Limited, Lauzon, Quebec - 1966
HULL NO.:	650
O.A. DIMENSIONS:	730' x 75' x 41'

This name is Algonkian and is applied by Indian tribes for "abode of the Great Spirit." According to Indian legend, it is the dwelling place of both the good spirit, "gitchi manitou" and the evil spirit "matchi manitou." There is no real literal translation of the word.

Manitooulin is the name of the largest island on freshwater in the world. It is largely inhabited by Algonquin Indians. The community of Little Current, Ontario formerly was the site of iron ore, coal and liquid product handling, but that is now ceased. A large limestone quarry at Meldrum Bay, on the western end of the island, is the main commercial activity today.

The Motor Vessel MANITOULIN sailed on its maiden trip July 8, 1966 with a cargo of manganese ore from Contrecoeur, Quebec to Ashtabula, Ohio. On December 13, 1966, it broke a limestone cargo record that had stood since 1953 when it loaded 22,446 gross tons at Port Colborne, Ontario for delivery to Cleveland,Ohio.

The ship is shown in the Welland Ship Canal, downbound below the Flight Locks, on October 30, 1997.

Motor Vessel Rt. Hon. PAUL J. MARTIN

OWNER:	Canada Steamship Lines, Inc.
BUILT:	Collingwood Shipyards, Collingwood, Ontario - 1973
HULL NO.:	203
O.A. DIMENSIONS:	740' x 78' x 48'5"
FORMER DATA:	Launched as H. M. GRIFFITH. Lengthened 10', widened 3', deepened 1'11" and given present name in 2000 at Port Weller Dry Docks, St. Catharines, Ontario.

The Rt. Honourable Paul Joseph James Martin was born in Ottawa, Ontario on June 23, 1903 and graduated from the University of Toronto with a B.A. degree, from Osgoode Hall with an M.A. degree and from Harvard University with an LL.M. degree in 1929. He made a life of public service and was bestowed many honors too numerous to mention. His son, Paul, is currently serving as Canada's finance minister in the federal government.

This self-unloader was launched in the fall of 1973 and sailed on its maiden voyage October 31st in ballast for Thunder Bay, Ontario where it loaded iron ore for Hamilton, Ontario.

The carrier is shown in this photograph exiting Lock 1 of the Welland Ship Canal on April 21, 2000. It was supposed to be enroute to Lake Ontario for sea trials following its rebuilding. Instead, it is shown being "Flushed out" of the lock by Seaway officials because it lost power of its engines while in the lock. Note seamen on the lock wall assisting.

Motor Vessel NANTICOKE

OWNER:	Canada Steamship Lines Inc.
BUILT:	Collingwood Shipyards, Collingwood, Ontario - 1980
HULL NO.:	218
O. A. DIMENSIONS:	730' x 75'8" x 46'6"

The Motor Vessel NANTICOKE takes its name from the newest steel plant site on North America. It is the "greenfield" plant put into operation in 1980 by Stelco, Inc., this firms largest iron ore shipper. The plant is the first new steel mill on the North American continent in over two decades. It changed its name, internally, from Lake Erie Development to Lake Erie Works at 11:58 PM on June 1, 1980 when the first steel was produced at the site.

The name Nanticoke is Iroquoian, from the six nation tribes, which means meandering stream. A small creek does just this through the area. The town of Jarvis is presently the nearest community, but the steel firm has acquired large tracts of land outside the basic steel plant for development of an industrial park, which over the years is sure to grow.

Deliveries by vessel to the site are by means of the 1-1/4 mile long continuous conveyor system built into Lake Erie. It is suited for self-unloaders only and has all the appropriate environmental safeguards. The M/V NANTICOKE sailed on its maiden voyage June 12, 1980, light from Collingwood, Ontario to Marquette, Michigan to load iron ore pellets. It is shown in West Neebish Channel, St. Mary's River on September 5, 1998.

Motor Vessel JEAN PARISIEN

OWNER:	Canada Steamship Lines Inc.
BUILT:	Davie Shipbuilding, Limited, Lauzon, Quebec - 1977
HULL NO.:	684
O. A. DIMENSIONS:	730' x 75' x 46'6"

The self-unloading bulk freight Motor Vessel JEAN PARISIEN was named posthumously in 1977 for Mr. Jean Parisien. He was the senior deputy chairman of Power Corporation of Canada, Limited when the decision to build this vessel was made and he died on February 20, 1976 in Montreal, Quebec.

Mr. Parisien was born in Plantagenet, Ontario on November 12, 1922. He received an M.B.A. degree from McGill University in 1945 and began work with Mr. Louis Desmarais at Sudbury, Ontario in the accounting firm of Desmarais and Parisien. In 1951 the team associated with Paul Desmarais is solving transportation management problems at Sudbury Bus Lines, Limited and, in 1959, formed Transportation Management Company. This led to senior positions in the conglomerate firm known most popularly today as "Power Corp." Mr. Parisien was actively in charge of financial analysis work in the firm when he died.

His namesake sailed on its maiden trip December 9, 1977 from Quebec City, light to Sandusky, Ohio to load coal for Hamilton, Ontario delivery. The ship is shown passing downbound in the West Neebish Channel, St. Mary's River, on July 23, 1998.

Motor Vessel TADOUSSAC (4)

OWNER: Canada Steamship Lines Inc.
BUILT: Collingwood Shipyards, Collingwood, Ontario—1969
HULL NO.: 192
O. A. DIMENSIONS: 730′ × 75′3″ × 42′

The Motor Vessel TADOUSSAC is shown above while downbound in the West Neebish Channel, St. Mary's River on May 30, 1976. It left Collingwood, Ontario October 2, 1969 on its maiden voyage enroute to Fort William, Ontario to load iron ore.

Tadoussac, Quebec is the namesake of this ship. It is the oldest settlement in Canada, having been visited by Jacques Cartier on September 1, 1535. It is now the county seat of Saguenay County and is located about one hundred-four miles north-east of Quebec City on the north shore of the St. Lawrence River where the Saguenay River joins the St. Lawrence.

In 1615 Recollet Jean Dolbeau built the first mission to the Indians there. It was taken over by the Jesuits in 1641. Tourist traffic to the scene dates from 1853 and has had much to do with the development of the area. Regular sailings used to be provided from Montreal and Quebec City, stopping at Tadoussac, to Port Alfred, Quebec, but these have now been discontinued. The name is Algonkin and, variously, means "breasts" because of the low rounded hills in the locale, or "meeting place of the waters," because of the confluence of the two large rivers at the site.

Steamer SOUTHDOWN CHALLENGER

OWNER:	Cement Transit Company
BUILT:	Great Lakes Engineering Works, Ecorse, Michigan - 1906
HULL NO.:	17
O.A. DIMENSIONS:	552'1" x 56' x 31'
FORMER DATA:	Launched as the bulk freighter WILLIAM P. SNYDER. Renamed ELTON HOYT II (1) in 1926. Renamed ALEX D. CHISHOLM in 1952. Renamed MEDUSA CHALLENGER in 1966. Converted to a self-unloading cement carrier at Manitowoc Shipbuilding, Incorporated, Manitowoc, Wisconsin in 1967. Given present name in 1999.

The first word in this ship's name is in reference to the parent owner of Cement Transit, that being SOUTHDOWN Cement Corporation. Southdown purchased Medusa Cement in early 1999 and all of its subsidiaries.

The new owner kept the second word - CHALLENGER because it seemed appropriate in the vein of challenging other cement firms in the Great Lakes region in moving finished cement and doing so as economically as possible.

The home port for finished cement origin is the large plant located at Charlevoix, Michigan on the eastern shore of Lake Michigan. The Steamer SOUTHDOWN CHALLENGER is shown in this photograph while it is unloading at the company's terminal in Manitowoc, Wisconsin during September 1999.

Barge SOUTHDOWN CONQUEST

OWNER:	Cement Transit Company
BUILT:	Manitowoc Shipbuilding Company, Manitowoc, Wisconsin - 1937
HULL NO.:	292
O.A. DIMENSIONS:	437'6" x 55'3" x 28'
FORMER DATA:	Launched as the powered tanker RED CROWN. Renamed AMOCO INDIANA in 1962. Converted to a cement-carrying barge, shortened 45'6", deepened 2'6" and renamed MEDUSA CONQUEST at Bay Shipbuilding Corporation, Sturgeon Bay, Wisconsin in 1987. Lengthened 17'9" with a new stern at Erie Marine, Enterprises, Erie, Pennsylvania in 1992. Given present name in 1999.

This bulk self-unloading barge was also acquired by SOUTHDOWN Cement in early 1999. The second word in the name was kept in reference to conquering the demands of the Great Lakes cement trade by this firm.

The barge has a belt conveyor serving 8 cargo holds which feeds a bucket elevator. In turn, this unloads onto an airflow boom conveyor of 48' length for overboard discharge into receiving hoppers located at the company's various marine terminals around the Great Lakes. The Barge SOUTHDOWN CONQUEST is shown while inbound with cement at Cleveland, Ohio on October 31, 1999 with the Tug SUSAN W. HANNAH on the stern.

Motor Vessel GEMINI

OWNER:	Cleveland Tankers (1991) Inc.
BUILT:	Levingston Shipbuilding Company, Orange, Texas - 1978
HULL NO.:	745
O. A. DIMENSIONS:	430' x 65' x 29'4"

Namesake of the tank Motor Vessel GEMINI is the constellation in the Northern Hemisphere which, because of the precession of the equinoxes, is now in the constellation Taurus. The two brightest stars of this constellation are named Castor and Pollux. These names come from Greek mythology and refer to the children of Leda. Shown as a figure, these two are joined together at the shoulder and the hip.

Gemini is also the third sign of the zodiac and literally means, the twins. In modern terminology, the name is most often connected with the U.S. space program wherein the first of the two-manned flights in space began the Gemini Project. The first flight took place on March 23, 1965 with Messrs. Virgil Grissom and John Young in the spacecraft.

The Motor Vessel GEMINI sailed on its maiden voyage August 23, 1978 light from Orange, Texas bound for Baytown, Texas where it loaded #6 fuel oil for Detroit, Michigan delivery. It became the largest American flag tanker on the Great Lakes with a capacity of 75,000 barrels. It is shown passing downbound in the West Neebish Channel, St. Mary's River, on July 19, 1990.

Motor Vessel SATURN (4)

OWNER:	Cleveland Tankers (1991) Inc.
BUILT:	S. B. A. Shipyards, Inc., Jennings, Louisiana - 1974
HULL NO.:	218
O. A. DIMENSIONS:	384'6" x 54'6" x 25'

The tank Motor Vessel SATURN (4) was constructed in a building program for these owners encompassing two modern motor vessels. Before completion of this hull, but when it was well along towards completion, management decided to name both vessels at once and in some sort of theme in keeping with the fleet names for ships being derived from celestial bodies or things relating thereto.

The Motor Vessel SATURN is shown while downbound in the West Neebish Channel, St. Mary's River on August 6, 1982.

In mythology Saturn was the father of Jupiter. The germane relationship of these ship names comes for the fact that when this vessel was ordered in 1972 business was on the upswing and the fleet needed larger and more modern ships to handle the business. As the months went by, it became evident that yet another ship was needed even before this Motor Vessel SATURN was delivered. The fact that this ship was "on the ways" bred a stronger need for tankers and the fleet managers complied to that need with another order for an even larger tanker. This tanker, then was seen as the "father" of the second ship much as Saturn was the father of Jupiter in mythology.

Motor Vessel AMELIA DESGAGNES

OWNER:	Desgagnes Transport, Inc.
BUILT:	Collingwood Shipyards, Collingwood, Ontario - 1976
HULL NO.:	210
O.A. DIMENSIONS:	355' x 49' x 30'6"
FORMER DATA:	Launched as the bulk freighter SOODOC (2). Converted to a crane-equipped bulk freighter at Swan Hunter Shipbuilders, Limited, Newcastle-on-Tyne, England in 1977. Given present name in 1990.

This ship name was selected from entries in a contest which was sponsored by the Desgagnes Groupe. The winning entry was submitted by Mr. Richard Bohay of Winnipeg, Manitoba. He is the chartering broker for the Desgagnes Fleet in that Canadian grain capital.

Contest rules stated that the name must be feminine, end with the letter "A" and be easily pronounceable in both English and French. Some 184 names were suggested by Desgagnes employees and senior management personnel were left with the decision to choose the winning name.

Use of the word DESGAGNES referenced the owning company. The first word stands for no person. Rather, it met the contest rules and thus was selected. The Motor Vessel AMELIA DESGAGNES is shown passing downbound in Sault Ste. Marie Harbor on August 5, 1994.

Motor Vessel CATHERINE DESGAGNES

OWNER:	Desgagnes Transport, Inc.
BUILT:	Hall, Russell & Company, Limited, Aberdeen, Scotland - 1962
HULL NO.:	894
O. A. DIMENSIONS:	410'3" x 55'6" x 31'
FORMER DATA:	Launched as GOSFORTH. Renamed THOROLD (4) in 1972. Given present name in 1985.

The bulk freight Motor Vessel CATHERINE DESGAGNES is shown while downbound in the West Neebish Channel, St. Mary's River, on June 10, 1990.

Namesake of this carrier is Ms. Catherine Desgagnes. She was born on February 9, 1975 in Levis, Quebec and is the daughter of Michel and France (nee Belsil) Desgagnes. Michel is a brother of Captain Yvan Desgagnes, president of this owning company.

Catherine lives with her parents in Levis where she attends school. It is not known whether she will become interested in the vessel business and take part in it. Her uncle, obviously, felt very warmly towards her when he renamed this motor vessel in her honor.

Motor Vessel CECILIA DESGAGNES

OWNER:	Desgagnes Transport, Inc.
BUILT:	Hollming Oy, Rauma, Finland - 1971
HULL NO.:	4196
O. A. DIMENSIONS:	374'10" x 54'10" x 34'6"
FORMER DATA:	Launched as CARL GROTHON. Lengthened 36' at Hollming Oy, Rauma, Finland in 1974. Renamed FEDERAL PIONEER in 1981. Given present name in 1985.

The Motor Vessel CECILIA DESGAGNES is a crane-equipped bulk freighter which can handle a wide variety of material and products. It is shown in this photograph nearing a berth on the St. Lawrence River in 1986.

Namesake of this carrier is Cecilia Desgagnes, wife of the late Mr. Roland Desgagnes, uncle of Captain Yvan Desgagnes who is president of this owning firm.

Cecilia was born September 1, 1912 in Les Eboulements, Quebec. Following her education, she worked in this family firm, serving as secretary for over 25 years. She was also in charge of a small electric power system for the town of St-Joseph-de-la-Rive, Quebec. She is now retired but does volunteer work from her home in St-Joseph-de-la-Rive.

A son, Mr. Guy Desgagnes, was port manager for Ports Canada in Chicoutimi, Quebec until 1989.

Motor Vessel JACQUES DESGAGNES

OWNER:	Desgagnes Transport, Inc.
BUILT:	Zaanlandse Scheepsbouw, Zaandam, Netherlands - 1960
HULL NO.:	484
O. A. DIMENSIONS:	208'10" x 36' x 14'
FORMER DATA:	Launched as LOUTRE CONSOL. Given present name in 1977.

The Motor Vessel JACQUES DESGAGNES has dual namesakes. Perhaps foremost is the elder Jacques who was born in Ducey, France on January 18, 1669. He was locally educated and came to North America with the French Army, arriving in Quebec City, Quebec on August 1, 1685. He served 14 years in the armed services, spending some time at Fort Pontchartrain which is now Detroit, Michigan. Upon retirement from the Army, Mr. Desgagnes borrowed some money and established a transportation service between Detroit and Montreal, Quebec. This occurred in the early 1700's. He led some of the trips himself, by canoe, between the two ports. The senior Jacques died in Montreal on August 5, 1714. It is believed by the present family that two of his sons began Groupe Desgagnes in 1810.

The second namesake of this bulk freight carrier is a brother of Mr. Yvan Desgagnes, president of the Desgagnes group of companies.

The Motor Vessel JACQUES DESGAGNES is shown while downbound in the West Neebish Channel, St. Mary's River, after having unloaded a cargo at Sault Ste. Marie, Ontario, on August 6, 1979.

Motor Vessel MARIA DESGAGNES

OWNER:	Desgagnes Transport, Inc.
BUILT:	Qui Xin Shipyard, Shanghai, China - 1999
HULL NO.:	QX 1255
O.A. DIMENSIONS:	393' 7" x 68'9" x 40'3"
FORMER DATA:	Launched as KILCHEM ASIA. Given present name in 1999.

After this tank vessel was being built for another owner, that firm defaulted on the contract agreement. The shipyard was left with a vessel nearly completed, but with no buyer. The yard sought a buyer for the ship worldwide. As events turned out, it was a ship that ideally suited Desgagnes Transport's vision of expansion in the liquid cargo market.

The carrier was acquired in the spring of 1999 and brought under Canadian registry. The tanker was immediately put to good use moving petroleum products into the Arctic region of Canada, with its maiden voyage being commenced June 26th from Quebec City, Quebec.

The ship name honors no one specifically. Rather the name was selected from numerous others in an employee's contest because of its mellifluous sound. The word DESGAGNES simply uses the common suffix in the fleet.

The vessel has a mid-summer draft carrying capacity of 93,500 barrels. It is shown while underway between Sillery, Quebec and Quebec City, Quebec on September 22, 1999 enroute to its formal dedication ceremony.

Motor Vessel MATHILDA DESGAGNES

OWNER:	Desgagnes Transport, Inc.
BUILT:	Davie Shipbuilding, Limited, Lauzon, Quebec - 1959
HULL NO.:	617
O. A. DIMENSIONS:	360' x 51' x 30'
FORMER DATA:	Launched as the bulk freighter ESKIMO. Converted to a package freighter at Davie Shipbuilding, Limited, Lauzon, Quebec in 1964. Converted to a crane equipped package freighter and given present name at Davie Shipbuilding, Limited, Lauzon, Quebec in 1985.

The package freight Motor Vessel MATHILDA DESGAGNES is shown while downbound in the Welland Ship Canal in 1986. It was the first vessel to use the new dock facility at Grande Anse, Quebec, on the Saguenay River on November 22, 1985. The site was created because it was on deepwater, as opposed to ports not far upstream, such as Port Alfred and Chicoutimi, Quebec, which were restricted in their harbor depths. On this historic, first arrival at the new facility, this carrier brought in 5,509 metric tons of coal to be used in processing ferrosilicon metal.

Namesake of this carrier was the grandmother of Captain Yvan Desgagnes, company president, on his father's side. Mathilda Desgagnes (nee Audet) was born April 1, 1880 in Les Eboulements, Quebec. She was locally educated and married Mr. Zelada Desgagnes in February, 1899. When her husband died in 1940, the family owned three vessels: MONT ST-JOSEPH, MONT NOTRE-DAME and J.Z. DESGAGNES. Mathilda personally owned the MONT NOTRE-DAME and operated it until 1955. She was also part owner in the Desgagnes companies along with J.A.Z., Maurice and Roland Desgagnes. Mathilda died May 30, 1964 in St. Joesph de la Rive, Quebec.

Motor Vessel MELISSA DESGAGNES

OWNER:	Desgagnes Transport, Inc.
BUILT:	Collingwood Shipyards, Collingwood, Ontario - 1975
HULL NO.:	207
O.A. DIMENSIONS:	355' x 49' x 30'6"
FORMER DATA:	Launched as the bulk freighter ONTADOC (2). Converted to a crane-equipped bulk freighter at Mount Royal-Walsh, Inc., Montreal, Quebec in 1989. Given present name in 1990.

The Motor Vessel MELISSA DESGAGNES sailed on its maiden voyage April 24, 1975 in ballast from Collingwood, Ontario to Sault Ste. Marie, Ontario to load a cargo of steel for delivery to Duluth, Minnesota.

The carrier mainly operated in the pig iron, scrap metal and side-port grain trades its first thirteen seasons. As some of this business dwindled, the decision was made by add cranes for assistance in cargo handling at ports where no such equipment existed. However, this did not prove worthwhile and the vessel was sold to this owner in 1990.

This vessel was named in the same contest among Desgagnes Groupe employees as was the AMELIA DESGAGNES, which was explained in the write-up of that vessel. In this case, the name was the suggestion of Mr. Paul Cote, General Manager of Corporate Sales and Marketing. The vessel is shown April 30, 1997 while inbound at Port Weller, Ontario, Welland Ship Canal.

Motor Vessel PETROLIA DESGAGNES

OWNER:	Desgagnes Transport, Inc.
BUILT:	Anker Lokken Verft Glommen, A.S., Fredrikstad, Norway - 1975
HULL NO.:	188
O. A. DIMENSIONS:	441'6" x 56'6" x 32'9"
FORMER DATA:	Launched as JORAVN. Renamed LIDO in 1979. Renamed EK-SKY in 1984. Given present name in 1998.

The tank Motor Vessel PETROLIA DESGAGNES is a sistership to the THALASSA DESGAGNES in virtually all respects. It has eight cargo tanks port and starboard, for a total of sixteen. Carrying capacity at its all-season loadline is 10,512 cubic meters with the tanks 98% full.

This vessel name was suggested by principals of Petro-Nav Inc. who are minority owners of the carrier. Thus, it diverts from the modern Desgagnes theme for selecting vessel names by contest among its employees.

The namesake is Petrolia, Ontario, 16 miles southeast of Sarnia, Ontario and Canada's first "oil capital." It is located on Bear Creek in Lambton County and was originally known as Enniskillen. It was renamed Petrolia in 1861 in honor of the discovery of rock oil. It was incorporated as a village in 1866 and as a town in 1873. The first of 15 oil refineries and drill holes were in operation by 1880.

The Motor Vessel PETROLIA DESGAGNES is shown passing upbound in the Welland Ship Canal on April 24, 1998.

Motor Vessel THALASSA DESGAGNES

OWNER:	Desgagnes Transport, Inc.
BUILT:	Anker Lokken Verft Glommen, A.S., Fredrikstad, Norway - 1976
HULL NO.:	189
O.A. DIMENSIONS:	441'6" x 56'6" x 32'9"
FORMER DATA:	Launched as ORINOCO. Renamed JOASLA in 1979. Renamed RIO ORINOCO in 1982. Given present name in 1993.

The Motor Vessel THALASSA DESGAGNES is a petroleum product tank vessel. It became the first tanker in the Desgagnes Fleet when it departed St. Romuald, Quebec February1, 1994 with a cargo of gasoline destined for Montreal, Quebec. During the interim period from its 1993 naming, the vessel was under reconstruction from a stranding accident.

The stranding occurred in foul weather when the ship was carrying asphalt. It stranded on the rocky shore of Anticosti Island in October 1990. Desgagnes won the salvage bidding on a "no cure, no pay" basis, and was successful in salvaging the carrier early in 1993.

Refurbishing work was done at MIL Davie's shipyard in Lauzon, Quebec. The tanker has a carrying capacity of 6,290 cubic meters. The common suffix DESGAGNES is used and THALASSA is a Greek word which means "the sea."

The Motor Vessel THALASSA DESGAGNES is shown passing upbound "on the level" of the Welland Ship Canal, below Lock #8, on October 29, 1997.

Motor Vessel JOHN R. EMERY

OWNER:	Erie Navigation Company
BUILT:	W. J. Kingston & Company, Buffalo, New York - 1905
HULL NO.:	None assigned.
O. A. DIMENSIONS:	140' x 33' x 14'
FORMER DATA:	Launched as the bulk freighter TRENTON. Converted to a self-unloading sandsucker at Great Lakes Engineering Works, River Rouge, Michigan in 1925. Given present name in 1928. Reconverted to a bulk freight sandsucker at Erie Sand and Gravel Company, Erie, Pennsylvania in 1959.

Mr. John Ritchie Emery christened his own namesake when he was ten years old and made a trip aboard on its maiden voyage. Mr. Emery was born at Detroit, Michigan on September 20, 1918 and is a graduate of the University of Michigan, having obtained a B.A. degree in 1940.

He began his career as an ordinary seaman on Great Lakes vessels and then went ashore as a salesman for a building supply and marine firm in Detroit. From 1943 to 1945 he served in the United States Navy, achieving the rank of lieutenant in 1945. He joined W. L. Emery Company as general manager that year and in 1948 became its president. From 1959 until 1966 he was director of the Great Lakes Seamen's Appeal Board. In 1966 he returned to W. L. Emery Company as president. The ship is shown outbound on a rare trip into Toledo, Ohio on June 20, 1994.

Motor Vessel DAY PECKINPAUGH

OWNER:	Erie Navigation Company
BUILT:	McDougall-Duluth Shipbuilding Company, Duluth, Minnesota—1921
HULL NO.:	50
O. A. DIMENSIONS:	254′ × 36′ × 14′
FORMER DATA:	Launched as the barge canal freighter I. L. I. 101. Renamed RICHARD J. BARNES in 1936. Rebuilt with new midbody and shortened 3′4″ at Todd Shipyards, Incorporated, Hoboken, New Jersey in 1946. Given present name in 1958. Converted to a self-unloading cement carrier at Erie Sand and Gravel Company, Erie, Pennsylvania in 1962.

Mr. Day Peckinpaugh, an elder statesman of the Great Lakes vessel industry, is the namesake of this ship. He was born at Wooster, Ohio on September 5, 1886 and was educated in the public schools. He died in Cleveland, Ohio on January 23, 1978.

He began his business career as an office boy at Mitchell & Company in Cleveland, Ohio in 1900. This firm was one of the largest vessel owners and agents at the time. In 1907 he joined W. S. & J. S. Manuel in the lake forwarding business, handling coal shipments on the Great Lakes. He became a partner in that firm in 1920 and in 1940 was named senior partner. Mr. Peckinpaugh still serves in that capacity. From 1961 to 1966 he was also president of the Buckeye Steamship Company and from 1966 until late 1967 was its chairman of the board. That firm is now out of business. This vessel's maiden trip was from Duluth, Minnesota June 3, 1921 with a cargo of wheat for New York, New York delivery.

Motor Vessel RICHARD REISS

OWNER:	Erie Sand Steamship Company
BUILT:	Great Lakes Engineering Works, River Rouge, Michigan - 1943
HULL NO.:	290
O.A. DIMENSIONS:	620'6" x 60'3" x 35'
FORMER DATA:	Launched as the bulk freighter ADIRONDACK. Renamed RICHARD J. REISS in 1943. Converted to a self-unloader at Manitowoc Shipbuilding, Incorporated, Manitowoc, Wisconsin in 1964. Given present name in 1986.

This vessel cleared Sandusky, Ohio with a cargo of coal on May 25, 1943 destined for delivery to Sheboygan, Wisconsin. That port was the corporate headquarters of the C. Reiss Coal Company at the time.

The namesake was Mr. Richard John Reiss who was born in Sheboygan on November 28, 1882. He graduated from Sheboygan High School and entered the family coal and vessel business. His first assignment was the St. Paul, Minnesota office where he learned the complexities of dealing with customers and satisfying their fuel needs.

Health reasons dictated his move to Colorado where he settled in Colorado Springs. He died there in 1956.

His namesake is shown departing Cleveland, Ohio on November 16, 1990. His middle initial was removed from the ship name by this owner because, using it, would have meant there were thirteen letters and that was not deemed to be a lucky thing.

Motor Vessel J. S. ST. JOHN

OWNER:	Erie Sand Steamship Company
BUILT:	Smith's Shipyard, Incorporated, Pensacola, Florida - 1945
HULL NO.:	117
O. A. DIMENSIONS:	174' x 32'2" x 15'
FORMER DATA:	Launched as the tanker USS-YO 178. Renamed LAKE EDWARD in 1951. Converted to a sandsucker and given present name at Niagara Industries, Incorporated, Erie Pennsylvania in 1967.

Namesake of this motor vessel is Mr. Joseph Scobell St. John who was born at Erie, Pennsylvania on September 30, 1903. He attended Carnegie Institute of Technology and began his career as a sailor on the F. D. UNDERWOOD. This vessel was a combination crane vessel and package freighter for the Great Lakes Transit Company.

In 1933 he obtained his master's papers and became Captain St. John. At this time he joined the Erie Sand Steamship Company fleet and sailed as captain for three years, coming ashore in 1936 as marine superintendent. He became manager of the fleet in 1939 and president in 1942. Captain St. John was elected chairman of the board of Erie Sand Steamship in 1964.

He had hobbies of raising cattle and horses. Capt. St. john died at Erie, Pennsylvania on January 11, 1983. His namesake is shown entering Erie Harbor in October 1996.

Barge METIS

OWNER:	Essroc Canada Inc.
BUILT:	Davie Shipbuilding, Limited Lauzon, Quebec - 1956
HULL NO.:	609
O. A. DIMENSIONS:	331' x 43'9" x 26'
FORMER DATA:	Launched as a powered bulk freighter. Lengthened 72' at Kingston Shipyards, Kingston, Ontario in 1959. Converted to a powered cement carrier at Kingston Shipyards, Kingston, Ontario in 1966. Converted to a cement-carrying barge by Great Lakes Ship Management, Toronto, Ontario in 1991.

The Barge METIS is named for a group of people who became a semi-Indian tribe on the prairies of Canada. They are not pure blooded Indian, but a mixture of Indian and European strains.

The word METIS is French and is derived from the Latin "miscere," meaning to mix. These people are offsprings of Canadian fur traders and have Ojibwa and Cree Indian, ancestry. Today, the group is mostly settled in the Red River Valley.

The Barge METIS is shown above in "ready to go" condition, just prior to its first departure since the noted conversion. The place is Toronto, Ontario and the date is May 2, 1991.

Motor Vessel STEPHEN B. ROMAN

OWNER:	Essroc Canada Inc.
BUILT:	Davie Shipbuilding, Limited, Lauzon, Quebec - 1965
HULL NO.:	652
O. A. DIMENSIONS:	488'9" x 56' x 35'6"
FORMER DATA:	Launched as the package freighter FORT WILLIAM. Converted to a cement carrier at Collingwood Shipyards, Collingwood, Ontario and given present name in 1983.

The namesake of this modern cement carrier was Mr. Stephen Boleslav Roman, K.C.S.G., LL.D., who was born on April 17, 1921 at Velky Ruskov, Slovakia. He was educated in the public schools and the Agricultural College. He moved to Canada in 1937 and worked on a farm in Port Perry, Ontario. He later worked in manufacturing plants at Oshawa, Ontario until serving in the Canadian Army in World War II until discharged in 1943. Until 1945, he worked for General Motors of Canada at Oshawa.

In 1946, Mr. Roman organized the Concord Mining Syndicate to develop oil and gas interests in Canada and the United States. In the early 1950's he acquired and developed the property now known as Denison Mines Limited at Elliot Lake, Ontario. This firm has become a diversified industrial complex in fields of oil, gas, uranium, potash, cement materials and other mining interests in the western world. Mr. Roman was chairman and the chief executive of Denison Mines, which owned 54% of this company, until his death in Toronto, Ontario on March 23, 1988. His namesake is shown approaching Lock 7 of the Welland Ship Canal on July 10, 1998.

Motor Vessel PRESQUE ISLE (2)

OWNER: GLF Great Lakes Corp.
BUILT: Barge: Erie Marine, Inc., Erie, Pennsylvania - 1973 (Hull) & Defoe Shipbuilding Company, Bay City, Michigan - 1972 (Bow) Tug: Halter Marine Services, Inc., New Orleans, Louisiana - 1973
HULL NO.: Barge: Hull-102, Bow-447; Tug: 322
O. A. DIMENSIONS: Barge: 974’6” x 104’7” x 46’6”; Tug: 153’3” x 54” x 31’3” Together: 1,000’ x 104’7” x 46’6”’

This tug/barge combination self-unloading bulk freighter is unique in Great Lakes history. It has a single name though its two parts are, necessarily, registered separately under Government documentation rules. It may also be confusing to the observer to add together the overall lengths of the tug and the barge and find that they do not add up to the 1,000 feet shown above. This is because the barge has a shelf in the stern on which the tug rides and becomes in effect, part of the combined unit.

The Motor Vessel PRESQUE ISLE is also unique in that it started its maiden voyage later than any vessel in Great Lakes history, departing Erie, Pennsylvania on December 16, 1973 upbound, light for Two Harbors, Minnesota where it took on a cargo of iron ore pellets for delivery to lower Lake Michigan.

The namesake of this tug/barge combination vessel was suggested in a contest at Erie Marine, Inc., by Mr. Richard E. Raleigh who was head of accounting in 1973. The name aptly pays tribute to the peninsula that protects the harbor at Erie, Pennsylvania in which this vessel was primarily built. The name was first used in North America in 1605 by Champlain and is of French derivation - *Presquile*, meaning, “almost or very near an island.” This vessel is shown above while downbound in the West Neebish Channel, St. Mary’s River on August 16, 1999.

Motor Vessel WOLF RIVER

OWNER:	Gravel & Lake Services Limited
BUILT:	Port Weller Dry Docks, Limited, St. Catharines, Ontario - 1956
HULL NO.:	19
O.A. DIMENSIONS:	349' x 43'6" x 25'6"
FORMER DATA:	Launched as TECUMSEH (2). Lengthened 90' at Canadian Vickers, Limited, Montreal, Quebec in 1959. Renamed NEW YORK NEWS (3) in 1967. Renamed STELLA DESGAGNES in 1986. Renamed BEAM BEGINNER in 1993. Given present name in 1995.

This 5,900 gross ton capacity bulk freighter was acquired by this owner at a sheriff's auction in the spring of 1995 when the Mexican interests which bought the vessel late in 1993 failed in their attempts to actually operate the carrier in off-lake trades.

The namesake reference is to the Wolf River in northern Ontario. It flows into Black Bay north-northeastward of Thunder Bay,Ontario. The river is not navigable by large craft, but was used formerly for movement of logs being brought to Black Bay for rafting from the hinterland.

The Motor Vessel WOLF RIVER is shown on its first voyage for this firm, inbound with pulpwood for Hallet Dock #8 in Superior, Wisconsin on June 30, 1998. The cargo was trans-shipped to a paper mill in Hayward, Wisconsin.

Steamer KINSMAN ENTERPRISE (2)

OWNER:	Great Lakes Associates, Inc.
BUILT:	American Ship Building Company, Lorain, Ohio - 1927
HULL NO..:	798
O.A. DIMENSIONS:	631' x 65' x 33'
FORMER DATA:	Launched as HARRY COULBY (2). Given present name in 1989.

This bulk freighter held the record for the largest iron ore cargo carried on the Great Lakes intermittently for 15 years. She and another carrier, now decommissioned, took turns bettering one another's records. On July 1, 1940, this carrier loaded 16,067 gross tons of iron ore at the Chicago & North Western Railway's dock in Ashland, Wisconsin to break the 16,000 gross ton barrier for the first time.

The vessel sailed on its maiden trip September 10, 1927 with a cargo of coal from Lorain, Ohio destined for delivery to Duluth, Minnesota. It is shown below on September 4, 1994 while downbound in the West Neebish Channel, St. Mary's River, with grain.

Until late 1997, this owner went by the name of Kinsman Lines. The company has been controlled by the Steinbrenner family for nearly a century. KINSMAN in this ship's name reflects this. The second word returns a name used in the fleet since 1965. Survival of a small, independent fleet has been an ENTERPRISE, the word being defined as "a project that is difficult, complicated or risky." The fleet is the only U.S. flag operator in the domestic grain trade at this time.

Steamer KINSMAN INDEPENDENT (3)

OWNER:	Great Lakes Associates, Inc.
BUILT:	Defoe Shipbuilding Company, Bay City, Michigan - 1952
HULL NO..:	422
O.A. DIMENSIONS:	642'3" x 67' x 35'
FORMER DATA:	Launched as CHARLES L. HUTCHINSON (3). Renamed ERNEST R. BREECH in 1962. Given present name in 1988.

This bulk freighter Steamer ERNEST R. BREECH was headed for the scrappers during the winter of 1987-1988 when Kinsman decided to acquire the ship for the grain trade. Vessels of this size were becoming few and far between and the Kinsman Fleet needed some replacement capacity for their aging ships. An agreement was made with the BREECH's owners, Ford Motor Company, and it became the property of Kinsman lines.

Comment about the name KINSMAN was made for the previous vessel. The second word in this ship's name reflects the fact that the fleet is INDEPENDENT from outside ownership and has continued to survive while other independent firms have passed from the Great Lakes scene. Grain from Duluth/Superior Harbor to Buffalo, New York occupies nearly 100% of this carrier's time.

The Steamer KINSMAN INDEPENDENT (3) is shown below while passing downbound in the West Neebish Channel, St. Mary's River, on May 28, 1995.

Barge SARAH SPENCER

OWNER: Great Lakes Transport Limited
BUILT: Manitowoc Shipbuilding, Incorporated, Manitowoc, Wisconsin - 1959
HULL NO..: 424
O.A. DIMENSIONS: 594'3" x 72' x 40'
FORMER DATA: Launched as the powered self-unloader ADAM E. CORNELIUS (3). Shortened 72'3" and converted to a self-unloading barge at Halifax Dartmouth industries, Limited, Halifax, Nova Scotia and renamed CAPT. EDWARD V. SMITH in 1989. Renamed SEA BARGE ONE in 1991. Given present name in 1996.

One might say that this vessel was "reborn" when it returned to Great Lakes service as SEA BARGE ONE in the spring of 1995. Owned by Mr. Allen L. Stevens of New Cannan, Connecticut, the barge and tug have been managed by Canada Steamship Lines, and used largely in the upper lakes grain trade. The trading routes have been mostly from Thunder Bay, Ontario to various United States and Canadian destinations.

The barge's name is taken from the two children of Mr. Stevens. Sarah was born in New York, New York on April 26. 1987 and her brother, Spencer, was born in that city on July 13, 1989. Both are currently attending elementary school.

The Barge SARAH SPENCER is shown in this photograph being pushed by the Tug ATLANTIC HICKORY at the head end of the Rock Cut in the West Neebish Channel, St. Mary's River, on July 24, 1996.

Barge IMPERIAL LACHINE (2)

OWNER:	Imperial Oil Limited
BUILT:	Port Weller Dry Docks Limited, St. Catharines, Ontario—1963
HULL NO.:	32
O. A. DIMENSIONS:	175′ × 36′ × 14′

The self-propelled Barge IMPERIAL LACHINE is a harbor tanker used in bunkering service and transfer service in the area of Montreal and Sorel, Quebec. It normally receives its cargo at the Montreal East refinery of this owning company.

This unit has only limited power of its own, utilizing outboard package power units of 750 shaft horsepower capacity. The barge has five individual tanks for the carriage of cargo and a carrying capacity of 9,415 barrels of fuel oil.

The first word of this ship name honors the owning company. This is the common first word of all ship names in the fleet. The specific namesake of this tank barge is the city of Lachine, Quebec. This is the famous suburb of Montreal, Quebec located near the Lachine Rapids in the St. Lawrence River and the western terminus of the former Lachine Canal which bypassed those rapids.

The land of the site was used by La Salle as the base point for his 1669 explorations. It had been granted him in 1666 by the Sulpicians. It is thought that the name was given by La Salle's men who dreamed of finding China in their push westward. The French "La Chine" means China. First settlers came to the spot in 1675. In 1689 many were massacred by Iroquois Indians, but later Lachine became the local headquarters for the Hudson's Bay Company. Today it is largely a residential community.

The ship is shown returning to its Montreal berth from a bunkering assignment on October 9, 1980.

Steamer ALPENA (2)

OWNER:	Inland Lakes Transportation, Inc.
BUILT:	Great Lakes Engineering Works, River Rouge, Michigan - 1942
HULL NO.:	287
O. A. DIMENSIONS:	519'6" x 67' x 35'
FORMER DATA:	Launched as the bulk freighter LEON FRASER. Shortened 120', converted to a self-unloading cement carrier and given present name at Fraser Shipyards, Inc., Superior, Wisconsin in 1991.

The cement-carrying Steamer ALPENA (2) is the largest on the Great Lakes in terms of its capacity. At mid-summer draft, the vessel's capacity is 13,900 gross tons. The steamer is shown while passing downbound in the West Neebish Channel, St. Mary's River on June 8, 1991. It is the vessel's first trip since conversion and it is enroute to its christening at Alpena, Michigan on June 10th.

This name was chosen because of the very large cement plant located in the city of Alpena, Michigan at which cargoes of this fleet are regularly loaded. It is also the city which is called headquarters for operations of this fleet.

Alpena has a current population of about 15,000 and is situated on Thunder Bay, an arm of Lake Huron. The community is a summer and winter resort area, with an annual winter carnival, good hunting and fishing areas within easy reach and many homes situated along its extensive shoreline. Alpena was first settled in 1835, was laid out in 1853 and incorporated as a city in 1871.

Steamer S. T. CRAPO

OWNER:	Inland Lakes Transportation, Inc.
BUILT:	Great Lakes Engineering Works, River Rouge, Michigan - 1927
HULL NO.:	256
O. A. DIMENSIONS:	402'6" x 60'3" x 29'

Mr. Stanford Tappan Crapo was a co-founder of Huron Portland Cement Company, along with Mr. J. B. Ford, and served as its secretary until his death on January 26, 1939. His namesake was the second vessel built from the keel up for Huron as a cement carrier. It is still a profitable ship and a perennial early opener of Great Lakes ports. It has a capacity of 47,000 barrels of cement.

Mr. Crapo was born in New Bedford, Massachusetts on June 13, 1865 and received his B.A. degree from Yale University in 1886. In many respects, Mr. Crapo was the father of Huron for thirty-two years, serving also as treasurer during that time. He was the only boss that most of the main office personnel ever knew, always accessible and always on the firing line. It was primarily his thrift and foresight that developed the unique character of Huron in the expansion of its plants and trading area over the Great Lakes region.

He was a man of many interests, a director and owner in widely diversified companies and for sixteen years, 1922–1938, he was a director of the Federal Reserve Bank of Chicago, District Seven.

His namesake is shown arriving at Muskegon, Michigan on April 18, 1991.

Steamer E. M. FORD

OWNER:	Inland Lakes Transportation, Inc.
BUILT:	Cleveland Shipbuilding Company, Cleveland, Ohio - 1898
HULL NO.:	30
O. A. DIMENSIONS:	428' x 50' x 28'
FORMER DATA:	Launched as the bulk freighter PRESQUE ISLE (1). Converted to a self-unloading cement carrier at Christy Corporation, Sturgeon Bay, Wisconsin and given present name in 1956.

The venerable Steamer E. M. FORD started a new career as a cement carrier on July 24, 1956 when it was christened in honor of Mr. Emory Moran Ford, then chairman of the board of Huron. Mr. Ford was born on April 19, 1906 at Detroit, Michigan and received his college education at Princeton University, graduating in 1928. He then went to work for the Michigan Alkali Company. In 1929 he was named a director of Huron Portland Cement Company and in 1933 became its treasurer and assistant secretary. On June 3, 1936 he was named vice president, on December 4, 1941 president and on January 27,1953 chairman of the board, serving in that capacity until May, 1959. He died at Chicago, Illinois June 5, 1971.

Mr. Ford carried on many activities both in industry and civic affairs. Concurrent with his chairmanship at Huron was the same position at Wyandotte Chemicals Corporation. He was a director or trustee of several other organizations.

This vessel is shown on arrival at Muskegon, Michigan at 2025 hours on April 17, 1991.

Steamer J. A. W. IGLEHART

OWNER:	Inland Lakes Transportation, Inc.
BUILT:	Sun Shipbuilding & Dry Dock Company, Chester, Pennsylvania - 1936
HULL NO..:	155
O.A. DIMENSIONS:	501'6" x 68'3" x 37'
FORMER DATA:	Launched as the tanker PAN-AMOCO. Renamed AMOCO in 1955. Renamed H. R. SCHEMM in 1960. Converted to a self-unloading cement carrier and given present name at American Ship Building Company, Chicago, Illinois in 1965.

The namesake of this cement carrier was Mr.Joseph Alexander Wilson Iglehart. He was born November 15, 1891 in Baltimore, Maryland and graduated from Cornell University in 1914. At that time he joined Brooks, Stokes & Company in Philadelphia, Pennsylvania in the stock brokerage business.

He was a partner in Brooks, Stokes after 1920 and also owned Iglehart & Company in the period 1921-1931. He became a partner in E. W. Hutton & Company in 1935 and rose to associate chairman of that firm. Mr. Iglehart was a limited partner in that firm at the time of his death in Lutherville, Maryland on November 16, 1979.

This was the first ship in the fleet to be equipped with belt conveyor unloading machinery in addition to the airslide boom and elevators. It is shown while downbound in the West Neebish Channel, St. Mary's River, on August 9, 1993.

Motor Vessel PAUL H. TOWNSEND

OWNER:	Inland Lakes Transportation, Inc.
BUILT:	Consolidated Steel Corporation, Limited, Wilmington, California - 1945
HULL NO.:	1328
O.A. DIMENSIONS:	477' x 50' x 29'
FORMER DATA:	Launched as the C1-M-AV1 type ship HICKORY COLL. Renamed COASTAL DELEGATE in 1946. Converted to a self-unloading cement carrier and given present name at Bethlehem Steel Company, Shipbuilding Division, Hoboken, New Jersey in 1952. Lengthened 106'3" at Great Lakes Engineering Works, Ashtabula, Ohio in 1958.

This cement carrier is named for Mr. Paul Henson Townsend who was born in Clermont, New Jersey on December 19, 1889. He received a B.A. degree from Yale University in 1918 and joined the Huron Portland Cement Company in 1919 as superintendent of plants and vessels. He became general manger of the firm in 1938, vice president on December 8, 1942 and president in 1953. Mr. Townsend served as chairman from 1959 until his retirement. He died in Detroit, Michigan on November 22, 1981.

Mr. Townsend served as a director of Huron Cement, Lake Carriers' Association, the Detroit Board of Commerce and other organizations. His namesake came into the lakes via the Mississippi River system and is shown here passing downbound in the West Neebish Channel, St. Mary's River, on August 2, 1997.

Motor Vessel JOSEPH L. BLOCK

OWNER:	Indiana Harbor Steamship Company
BUILT:	Bay Shipbuilding Corporation, Sturgeon Bay, Wisconsin - 1976
HULL NO.:	715
O. A. DIMENSIONS:	728' x 78' x 45'

The self-unloading Motor Vessel JOSEPH L. BLOCK honored Mr. Joseph Leopold Block as its namesake, He was born in Chicago, Illinois on October 6, 1902 and attended Cornell University in the period 1920-1922. He then joined the sales staff of Inland Steel and rose to become assistant vice president in 1927.

He was elected vice president and a director in 1930, vice president - sales in 1936 and vice chairman of the board in 1949. Mr. Block was elected president of Inland Steel in 1953, chief executive officer in 1956 and was chairman of the company's board of directors until May 1, 1975. Mr. Block died in Chicago in November 17, 1992.

His namesake sailed on its maiden trip August 15, 1976 in ballast from Sturgeon Bay, Wisconsin to Escanaba, Michigan to load a cargo of iron ore pellets which totaled 32,607 gross tons. It was delivered to the company's steelmaking site at Indiana Harbor (East Chicago), Indiana. The ship is shown while upbound in the Middle Neebish Channel, St. Mary's River, with flux stone from Port Inland, Michigan to Duluth, Minnesota on August 10, 1999

Steamer EDWARD L. RYERSON

OWNER:	Indiana Harbor Steamship Company
BUILT:	Manitowoc Shipbuilding, Incorporated, Manitowoc, Wisconsin - 1960
HULL NO.:	425
O. A. DIMENSIONS:	730' x 75' x 39'

Mr. Edward Larned Ryerson came from a family which had long been involved in the iron and steel business, even from Colonial times. He was born in Chicago, Illinois on December 3, 1886 and was educated at Yale University, receiving a Ph.B. degree in 1908.

Mr. Ryerson had been president of the country's largest steel service center, Joseph T. Ryerson & Son, Inc., when it was merged into Inland Steel in 1935. He then became vice chairman of the board of Inland Steel. From 1940 until his retirement in 1953, he was chairman of the board of both Inland Steel and his original company.

In 1958, Mr. Ryerson was the chief delegate from the United States of various steel and ore mining firms visiting the U.S.S.R. He was also a director or trustee of innumerable public service councils during his retirement years. He died in Chicago on August 2, 1971.

The EDWARD L. RYERSON sailed August 4, 1960 in ballast from Manitowoc to Escanaba, Michigan on its maiden voyage to load iron ore for Indiana Harbor, Indiana. It is shown below on December 10, 1998, enroute to lay-up, in the Sturgeon Bay Canal. The vessel did not operate in 1999.

Steamer WILFRED SYKES

OWNER:	Indiana Harbor Steamship Company
BUILT:	American Ship Building Company, Lorain, Ohio - 1949
HULL NO.:	866
O. A. DIMENSIONS:	678' x 70' x 37'
FORMER DATA:	Launched as a bulk freighter. Converted to a self-unloader at Fraser Shipyards, Incorporated, Superior, Wisconsin in 1975.

The prototype of today's lake vessel is the Steamer WILFRED SYKES. It was the largest and most powerful ship ever constructed for Great Lakes commerce when it was built and is still one of the sleekest in appearance.

The Steamer WILFRED SYKES lost no time in setting new iron ore cargo records and did so three times in 1950. She broke her own record quite a number of times before achieving the top record of 21, 223 gross tons on August 27, 1952. The cargo was loaded at the Great Northern Railway's Allouez docks for Indiana Harbor, Indiana.

Mr. Wilfred Sykes, for whom the ship is named, was born in Palmerston, New Zealand on December 3, 1883. He attended Melbourne University in Australia and worked as an electrical engineer in Germany and the United States for Westinghouse prior to joining Inland Steel Company in 1932. He was largely responsible for the conversion of the equipment at Indiana Harbor Works from steam to electrical power. In 1941 he became president of Inland Steel and retained that position until retirement in 1949. He died at San Francisco, California May 2, 1964.

This photograph of the freighter was taken August 2, 1999 while the ship is being loaded with taconite pellets at Escanaba, Michigan. The SYKES sailed on its maiden trip April 19, 1950 with coal from Toledo, Ohio for Indiana Harbor, Indiana.

Motor Vessel JAMES R. BARKER

OWNER:	Interlake Steamship Company
BUILT:	American Ship Building Company, Lorain, Ohio - 1976
HULL NO.:	905
O. A. DIMENSIONS:	1004' x 105' x 50'

The self-unloading Motor Vessel JAMES R. BARKER became the largest carrier on the Great Lakes when it went into service on August 8, 1976, departing Cleveland, Ohio light for Taconite Harbor, Minnesota to load iron ore at 0005 hours.

Namesake of this fine ship is Mr. James Rex Barker. He was born in Cleveland, Ohio on August 3, 1935 and graduated from Columbia University with a B.A. degree in 1957. Following service in the Coast Guard until 1961, he returned to college and received an M.B.A. degree from Harvard University in 1963. At this time he joined the marine department of Pickands Mather & Co. and remained there until leaving in 1967 to join Harbridge House, Inc., transportation consultants. In 1969 Mr. Barker joined friends to form their own consulting firm, Temple, Barker & Sloane which firm was retained by Moore McCormack to solve their difficulties. Mr. Barker's solution was so good that in 1971 he became leader of the company and its subsequent subsidiaries. He resigned in January, 1987 to acquire the operation of the marine-related assets of his former company.

This vessel, longest on the Great Lakes in 1976, is shown while downbound in the West Neebish Channel, St. Mary's River, on August 13, 1987.

Steamer CHARLES M. BEEGHLY

OWNER:	Interlake Steamship Company
BUILT:	American Ship Building Company, Toledo, Ohio—1959
HULL NO.:	193
O. A. DIMENSIONS:	806′ × 75′ × 37′6″
FORMER DATA:	Launched as the bulk freighter SHENANGO II. Given present name in 1967. Lengthened 96′ at Fraser Shipyards, Inc., Superior, Wisconsin in 1972. Converted to a self-unloader at Fraser Shipyards, Inc., Superior, Wisconsin in 1981.

The native Ohioan for whom this ship is named is Mr. Charles Milton Beeghly. He was born at Bloomville, Ohio on October 6, 1908 and graduated from Ohio Wesleyan University in 1930 with a B.A. degree.

Mr. Beeghly started his business career as a clerk for the Metal Carbides Company in New Jersey. After two other posts, he joined Cold Metal Products Company in 1935 as a salesman. He rose to become vice president and a director of that firm in 1946 and served until the business was sold in 1957. In that year he became president of the Strip Steel Division of Jones & Laughlin Steel Corporation and also a director of Jones & Laughlin. Named executive vice president of Jones & Laughlin in 1958, he was elected president in 1960 and in 1963 became chairman of the boards. He retains these positions at the present time.

Mr. Beeghly has been active in many community affairs. His namesake is shown inbound in the Black River at Lorain, Ohio on May 16, 1987. It, thus, became the largest ship to transit that river with cargo.

Steamer ELTON HOYT 2nd (2)

OWNER:	Interlake Steamship Company
BUILT:	Bethlehem Steel Corporation, Shipbuilding Division, Sparrows Point, Maryland—1952
HULL NO.:	4512
O. A. DIMENSIONS:	698′6″ × 70′ × 37′
FORMER DATA:	Launched as a bulk freighter. Lengthened 72′ at American Ship Building Company, Chicago, Illinois in 1957. Converted to a self-unloader at American Ship Building Company, Toledo, Ohio in 1980.

Mr. Elton Hoyt 2nd is this bulk freighter's namesake. He was born on June 13, 1888 at Cleveland, Ohio and graduated from Yale University in 1911. He then became an iron ore salesman with Pickands, Mather & Company.

He was named a partner of Pickands, Mather in 1922 and gave great impetus to the increasing integration of the industry by bringing steel firms together in ownership of mines. Mr. Hoyt took over the marine department of Pickands, Mather in 1929 and also became a managing partner of the firm. In 1939 he became senior managing partner and president of Interlake Steamship Company. He died in Cleveland, Ohio on March 16, 1955 after a most productive career.

Mr. Hoyt promoted the use of taconite as a source of rich iron ore and was a moving force in the $300,000,000 development of Taconite Harbor and Hoyt Lakes, Minnesota. He served as a director of numerous firms in the mining, ore and steel industries. He enjoyed horseback riding and had headed a Yale scholarship committee. His namesake is shown above while downbound in the West Neebish Channel, St. Mary's River on June 22, 1988.

Steamer HERBERT C. JACKSON

OWNER:	Interlake Steamship Company
BUILT:	Great Lakes Engineering Works, River Rouge, Michigan - 1959
HULL NO.:	302
O. A. DIMENSIONS:	690' x 75' x 37'6"
FORMER DATA:	Launched as a bulk freighter. Converted to a self-unloader at Defoe Shipbuilding Company, Bay City, Michigan in 1975.

Mr. Herbert Cooper Jackson was born in Cleveland, Ohio on March 27, 1894 and graduated from Yale University with a B.A. degree in 1916. He joined Pickands Mather & Company the same year. After serving in various positions, he was elected a partner in 1942. During the period 1955-1960, he was the managing partner.

Mr. Jackson was elected executive vice president in 1960 and retained that title until retiring in December 1962 after forty-six years of service. He remained a director of the company until 1965 and died in Cleveland on December 1, 1981.

He was a director of the Central National Bank, the American Mining Congress and the American Iron Ore Association. He was keenly respected for his knowledge of mining taxation on both national and state levels.

The Steamer HERBERT C. JACKSON is shown while passing downbound in the West Neebish Channel, St. Mary's River, on July 14, 1994.

Motor Vessel MESABI MINER

OWNER:	Interlake Steamship Company
BUILT:	American Ship Building Company, Lorain, Ohio - 1977
HULL NO.:	906
O. A. DIMENSIONS:	1004′ x 105′ x 50′

This self-unloading bulk freighter was the second vessel commissioned in an initial two-ship building program for these owners for the "second half" and beyond the Twentieth Century's needs for cargo carriers. It was named in honor of the people of the Mesabi Iron Range who had encouraged the development of the mining industry in Minnesota. More particularly, it meant to honor those men and women of the area who helped develop the resources of Pickands Mather & Co., managers of this fleet.

Since 1883 Pickands Mather & Co. has had a stake in the development of the Mesabi Range. Through the ownership of properties and the development of resources it has become a major producer of iron ore pellets for the steel industry from this source as well as around the world. It was deemed apropos to name this ship in honor of the long and successful relationship between the range and the company when this vessel took its name. From 1853 the iron range has been variously spelled "Mesaba," "Missabay," and "Missabe." The official spelling, as used in this ship name, was adopted by the U. S. Government in 1906.

This vessel sailed on its maiden voyage light from Lorain, Ohio June 7, 1977 to Duluth, Minnesota and is shown above while upbound in the St. Clair River on April 25, 1987.

Motor Vessel PAUL R. TREGURTHA

OWNER:	Interlake Steamship Company
BUILT:	American Ship Building Company, Lorain, Ohio - 1981
HULL NO.:	909
O. A. DIMENSIONS:	1,013'6" x 105' x 56'
FORMER DATA:	Launched as WILLIAM J. DELANCEY. Given present name in 1990.

This self-unloader became the largest ship ever to sail the Great Lakes when it departed Lorain on May 10, 1981 in ballast for Silver Bay, Minnesota to load iron ore pellets. It remains the largest today and is the flagship of the Interlake Fleet.

Namesake of the carrier is Mr. Paul Richard Tregurtha. He was born in Orange, New Jersey on September 27, 1935 and graduated with a B.M.E. degree from Cornell University in 1958. He then attended the Harvard Business School where he met James R. Barker in 1963. The pair became friends and business associates almost immediately.

He was chairman of Moore McCormack Resources, Inc. when that firm was bought out in 1988, then he became a 50% owner of Mormac Marine Group, Inc. and chairman of its board of directors. He is also the current vice chairman of Interlake Steamship.

The Motor Vessel PAUL R. TREGURTHA is shown passing downbound in the West Neebish Channel, St. Mary's River, on September 3, 1994.

Barge PATHFINDER (3)

OWNER:	Interlake Transportation, Inc.
BUILT:	Great Lakes Engineering Works, River Rouge, Michigan - 1953
HULL NO.:	298
O. A. DIMENSIONS:	606'2" x 70' x 36'
FORMER DATA:	Launched as the powered bulk freighter J. L. MAUTHE. Converted to a self-unloading barge, shortened 40'10" and given present name at Bay Shipbuilding Corporation, Sturgeon Bay, Wisconsin in 1998.

Since the early 1980's, this carrier was utilized mainly in the domestic grain trade, but was laid-up by the late 1980's for lack of sufficient grain business. A new lease on life was given in 1998 with the above conversion. The combined overall length of the vessel and its usual pusher-tug is 700'2".

The use of the name PATHFINDER brings back to the Interlake Fleet a name which was on one of their former vessels during the period 1925-1963. Prior to that, it was carried on the whaleback PATHFINDER (1) which had been built in 1892.

The word PATHFINDER means "one that discovers a way." It was the hope and plan of management that this newly-created vessel would do just that in Great Lakes commerce. The word itself stems from the famous book by novelist James Fenimore Cooper who grew up in central New York state in his book entitled *The Pathfinder* published in 1840.

The vessel is shown while inbound with limestone at Cleveland, Ohio on June 24, 1998.

Barge KELLSTONE 1

OWNER:	Kellstone, Inc.
BUILT:	Todd Shipyards Corporation, Houston, Texas - 1957
HULL NO.:	180
O. A. DIMENSIONS:	350' x 60' x 22'6"
FORMER DATA:	Launched as the deck barge M-211. Lengthened 50', deepened 3'6" and converted to a pipe-laying hopper barge at Avondale Marine Ways, Inc., Avondale, Louisiana in 1959. Renamed VIRGINIA in 1981. Converted to a self-unloading hopper barge and given present name at Kellstone, Inc., Sandusky, Ohio in 1992.

The Barge KELLSTONE I and Tug FRANK PALLADINO, JR. sailed on their maiden voyage December 8, 1992 with a cargo of limestone from Kelley's Island, Ohio to Cleveland, Ohio. The loading port for the quarry on Kelley's Island had been largely inactive since the mid-1960's until the property was acquired by this owner in 1989. Quarrying had begun on the island in 1848 and was brought to full production by the Kelley Island Lime and Transport Company in the 1880's. Messrs. Webb, Kelley and Huntington were the first to begin mining and shipping operations.

The Barge KELLSTONE I is shown utilizing its unusual retractable unloading boom at the River Dock in Cleveland, Ohio on May 17, 1993.

Motor Vessel GREAT LAKES/MICHIGAN

OWNER:	Keystone Great Lakes, Inc.
BUILT:	Bay Shipbuilding Corporation, Sturgeon Bay, Wisconsin - 1982
HULL NO.:	Barge: 713 Tug: 732
O. A. DIMENSIONS:	Barge: 414' x 60' x 30'; Tug: 115' x 34' x 16' Together: 454' x 60' x 30'
FORMER DATA:	Launched as AMOCO GREAT LAKES/MICHIGAN. Given present name in 1985.

The tug-barge combination tanker Motor Vessel GREAT LAKES/MICHIGAN was the first such integrated unit placed in Great Lakes service in modern times. Over the years, many tug and barge combinations have been utilized in both Great Lakes and New York State Barge Canal trade patterns, but none of these carriers had so great a capacity or could be operated as one hull. At 75,000 barrels of gasoline capacity, this carrier has almost twice the capacity and efficiency of two of the former powered tankers in the fleet.

This operating company came into being as a result of the BP Amoco merger. When the tug-barge was placed into this fleet late in 1985, the name change was made. The Great Lakes in their entirety, along with the state of Michigan, are honored in this name. Major activity of the fleet is centered on delivery points in Michigan.

The Motor Vessel GREAT LAKES/MICHIGAN is shown while downbound in the West Neebish Channel, St. Mary's River on June 5, 1986.

Motor Vessel ENGLISH RIVER

OWNER:	Lafarge Canada, Inc.
BUILT:	Collingwood Shipyards, Collingwood, Ontario - 1961
HULL NO.:	171
O. A. DIMENSIONS:	404'3" x 60' x 36'6"
FORMER DATA:	Launched as a package freighter. Converted to a self-unloading cement carrier at Port Arthur Shipbuilding Company, Thunder Bay, Ontario in 1974.

The Motor Vessel ENGLISH RIVER takes its name from an inland river in the province of New Brunswick. It was a river of historic importance as part of the water route to the south that was used by early fur traders and explorers in opening up territory for settlement.

The river has minor importance today as far as commercial trade is concerned. It flows from the town of McAdam, New Brunswick to the Atlantic Ocean and has been integral to the development of lower New Brunswick. Captivating scenes await tourists along the river's path.

This cement company owner has primary production and distribution facilities at Bath, Heron Bay, Toronto and Whitefish, Ontario on the Canadian side of the Great Lakes.

The Motor Vessel ENGLISH RIVER is shown while upbound "on the level" of the Welland Ship Canal on August 23, 1998.

Motor Vessel INTEGRITY

OWNER:	Lafarge Corporation
BUILT:	Barge: Bay Shipbuilding Corporation, Sturgeon Bay, Wisconsin - 1996
	Tug: Halter Marine, Moss Point, Mississippi - 1976
HULL NO.:	Barge: 740; Tug: 499
O. A. DIMENSIONS:	Barge: 460' x 70' x 37'
	Tug: 149'6" x 40' x 22'
	Together: 543'6" x 70' x 37'

When the tug/barge INTEGRITY/JACKLYN M. was commissioned in July 1996, it marked the first new U.S.-flag capacity built for Great Lakes service in more than 14 years. The vessel also reflected significant forward movement in the technology for tug/barge transportation.

The barge is equipped with a high degree of automation. It has a bow thruster and a carrying capacity at a draft of 26'6" of 17,600 net tons of cement.

Lafarge conducted a contest among all of its United States cement group employees to select a name for the barge. A total of 330 entries were received. Of these, one employee each from Nashville, Tennessee and Whitehall, Pennsylvania suggested the name INTEGRITY. Their reasoning was to have the name exemplify their perception of the high quality and <u>integrity</u> of Lafarge's products and service.

The combined unit INTEGRITY/JACKLYN M. is shown above on its sea trials on Green Bay, Lake Michigan prior to entering service.

Steamer BADGER (2)

OWNER:	Lake Michigan Carferry Service, Inc.
BUILT:	Christy Corporation, Sturgeon Bay, Wisconsin - 1953
HULL NO.:	370
O. A. DIMENSIONS:	410'6" x 59'6" x 24'

The carferry and passenger Steamer BADGER (2) is shown departing from Ludington, Michigan on July 4, 1992. It is enroute to Manitowoc, Wisconsin.

The vessel was named in reference to the University of Wisconsin whose mascot is the animal of this name. The State of Wisconsin also goes by the name of the "Badger State."

The animal gets its name from the fact that a sort of badge is visible in its markings on the head. The badger has a narrow white stripe that runs from between its eyes onto its back. It is found on open plains, prairies and deserts.

The Steamer BADGER (2) was assigned an all-season draft of 18'7". It has a capacity of 180 automobiles and is licensed to transport 520 passenger, plus crew. The ship is the only regularly scheduled passenger service on the Great Lakes in waters of the United States, except for short-haul ferries for passengers only or small ferries which carry both passengers and automobiles up to a maximum of 44 cars.

Steamer KAYE E. BARKER

OWNER:	Lakes Shipping Company, Inc.
BUILT:	American Ship Building Company, Toledo, Ohio - 1952
HULL NO.:	189
O. A. DIMENSIONS:	767' x 70' x 36'
FORMER DATA:	Launched as the bulk freighter EDWARD B. GREENE. Lengthened 120' at Fraser Shipyards, Inc., Superior, Wisconsin in 1976. Converted to a self-unloader at American Ship Building Company, Toledo, Ohio in 1981. Renamed BENSON FORD (3) in 1985. Given present name in 1989.

Namesake of this self-unloading bulk freighter is Mrs. Kaye Elizabeth Barker. She was born November 1, 1935 in Chicago, Illinois and received a Master of Social Work degree from Simmons College in 1963.

She married Mr. James Rex Barker in 1957 and is the mother of three children. Mrs. Barker has strong interest in families and children and her social work in numerous programs exemplifies this commitment. In addition to these activities, she is a director of the Interlake Holding Company and the Mormac Marine Group. She also enjoys sailing, tennis, swimming and photography.

This vessel was the flagship of the Cleveland-Cliffs Fleet from its commissioning until being sold to the Ford Motor Company in 1985. It is shown in this photograph while downbound in the West Neebish Channel, St. Mary's River, on August 30, 1997.

Steamer JOHN SHERWIN (2)

OWNER:	Lakes Shipping Company, Inc.
BUILT:	American Ship Building Company, Toledo, Ohio - 1958
HULL NO.:	192
O. A. DIMENSIONS:	806' x 75' x 37'6"
FORMER DATA:	Lengthened 96' at Fraser Shipyards, Inc., Superior, Wisconsin in 1973.

This bulk freighter is named for Mr. John Sherwin who was born in Cleveland, Ohio on April 18, 1901. He graduated from the Sheffield Scientific School of Yale University with a B.S. degree in 1923 and joined the Union Trust Company in Cleveland.

In 1927, Mr. Sherwin was elected vice president of Union Trust and, in 1928, he became president of the Midland Bank of Cleveland. He was elected president of the Cleveland Trust Company in 1932 but resigned in 1942 to become a partner in Pickands Mather & Company and a vice president of its Interlake Steamship Company.

Mr. Sherwin was the senior managing director in 1955 and president in 1960. He was elevated to chairman in 1965 and continued in that capacity until Pickands Mather was sold to Diamond Shamrock Corporation in December 1968. He died in 1993.

The Steamer JOHN SHERWIN (2) sailed on its maiden trip May 4, 1958 in ballast from Cleveland to Taconite Harbor, Minnesota to load iron ore pellets. It is shown in lay-up status at Superior, Wisconsin on September 10, 1995, having last run in 1981.

Steamer LEE A. TREGURTHA

OWNER: Lakes Shipping Company, Inc.
BUILT: Bethlehem Shipbuilding and Drydock Company, Sparrows Point, Maryland - 1942
HULL NO.: 4378
O. A. DIMENSIONS: 826' x 75' x 39'
FORMER DATA: Launched as the tanker SAMOSET. Completed as the tanker CHIWAWA. Rebuilt, lengthened 228'3", converted to a bulk freighter with new midbody and renamed WALTER A. STERLING at American Ship Building Company, Lorain, Ohio in 1961. Lengthened 96' at American Ship Building Company, Lorain, Ohio in 1976. Converted to a self-unloader at American Ship Building Company, Lorain, Ohio in 1978. Renamed WILLIAM CLAY FORD (2) in 1985. Given present name in 1989.

Namesake of this self-unloading bulk freighter is Mrs. Dorothy Lee Anderson Tregurtha. She was born February 5, 1937 in Lake Forest, Illinois and attended local schools before attending Cornell University to study architecture.

Mrs. Tregurtha married Mr. Paul R. Tregurtha in 1958. He is an owner of Lakes Shipping Company, Interlake Steamship Company and Mormac Marine Group, Inc., all headquartered in Stamford, Connecticut. Mrs. Tregurtha has been active in civic and educational organizations and charitable activities for some time.

Her namesake is shown while passing downbound in the West Neebish Channel, St. Mary's River, on July 19, 1989.

Motor Vessel CUYAHOGA

OWNER:	Lower Lakes Towing Ltd.
BUILT:	American Ship Building Company, Lorain, Ohio - 1943
HULL NO.:	828
O. A. DIMENSIONS:	620' x 60' x 35'
FORMER DATA:	Launched as the bulk freighter J. BURTON AYERS. Converted to a self-unloader at American Ship Building Company, Toledo, Ohio in 1974. Given present name in 1995.

This vessel was one of sixteen "Maritime" class carriers built in 1943 to aid Great Lakes transportation of raw materials for World War II. It is one of just two remaining and sailed on its maiden voyage August 19, 1943 in ballast to Duluth, Minnesota to take on a cargo of iron ore.

Sold to this owner on August 1, 1995, after over a decade of idleness, the handsome vessel was refurbished and departed Sarnia, Ontario in mid-November to begin its new role under Canadian registry. It is shown here while unbound at Cleveland, Ohio on November 16, 1995 with its first payload of limestone. The cargo was loaded at Meldrum Bay, Ontario and unloaded at the CBS #2 dock.

The carrier took its name from the Cuyahoga River on which waterway this photograph was taken. Much of the business lined up for the ship brings it to the river frequently. The namesake meaning of CUYAHOGA is Indian for "crooked river." The Cuyahoga certainly lives up to its name as it winds through "the Flats" of the city.

Steamer SAGINAW (3)

OWNER: Lower Lakes Towing Ltd.
BUILT: Manitowoc Shipbuilding, Incorporated, Manitowoc, Wisconsin - 1953
HULL NO.: 417
O. A. DIMENSIONS: 639'3" x 72' x 36'
FORMER DATA: Launched as JOHN J. BOLAND (3). Given present name in 1999.

This self-unloader took its initial cargo on September 25, 1953 when it loaded limestone at Port Inland, Michigan for lower lakes delivery. It flew the flag of American Steamship Company until late 1999 when the vessel was sold to this owner.

Since this company acquired its first self-unloader in 1995, and business was found to fully occupy that ship's capacity, the firm actively sought another carrier to satisfy customer demands. Following a definite statement that the vessel was no longer needed in the American Steamship Fleet, a deal was struck and the Lower Lakes management team fulfilled its wish.

The SAGINAW (3) has a carrying capacity of 20,200 gross tons at a mid-summer draft of 26'2". It was towed from Superior, Wisconsin in late October and refurbished, registered in Canada and renamed by December. The namesake reference is to the Saginaw River of Michigan. Its many docks are the second highest destination points of the fleet. The SAGINAW (3) is shown upon its arrival at the Lafarge Construction Materials quarry in Meldrum Bay, Ontario on its first trip for this owner on December 5, 1999. The cargo was destined for Marysville, Michigan.

Motor Vessel D. C. EVEREST

OWNER:	McKeil Marine Limited
BUILT:	Kingston Shipyards Division, Kingston, Ontario - 1953
HULL NO.:	45
O. A. DIMENSIONS:	259' x 43'6" x 21'
FORMER DATA:	Launched as the crane-equipped woodpulp bulk freighter D. C. EVEREST. Converted to a crane-equipped bulk freighter at Ship Repairs & Supplies Limited, Toronto, Ontario and renamed CONDARRELL in 1981. Renamed D. C. EVEREST, for the second time, in 1988.

After only short use following the above-noted conversion in 1981, this vessel laid idle in Toronto until being acquired by these owners in 1986. The firm is primarily in the towing and salvage business, but is also quite active in sand dredging and any kind of general purpose haulage for which their tugs, ships and barges are suited.

As events unfolded, management of this firm determined to refit this vessel to be used for any general purpose haulage, but especially for using the crane for any salvage work which may be needed.

Namesake of this carrier was Mr. David Clark Everest who was born October 13, 1883 in Pine Grove, Michigan. He worked for Bryant Paper Company 1900-02, Munising Paper Company 1902-07 and joined Marathon Paper Mills Company in 1909 at Neenah, Wisconsin. He was chairman of the board of Marathon from 1950 through retirement in 1952. His namesake is shown, with a fresh coat of paint, in Hamilton, Ontario harbor on September 22, 1988.

Steamer ARMCO

OWNER:	Oglebay Norton Company, Marine Transportation
BUILT:	American Ship Building Company, Lorain, Ohio - 1953
HULL NO.:	870
O. A. DIMENSIONS:	767' x 70' x 36'
FORMER DATA:	Launched as a bulk freighter. Lengthened 120' at Fraser Shipyards, Inc., Superior, Wisconsin in 1974. Converted to a self-unloader at Bay Shipbuilding Corporation, Sturgeon Bay, Wisconsin in 1982.

The Steamer ARMCO is named for what was formerly called Armco Steel Corporation. It honors the long-standing hauling commitment by Oglebay Norton to transport Armco's iron ore on the Great Lakes.

Armco was incorporated June 27, 1917 in Ohio as The American Rolling Mill Company and adopted the Armco name on April 17, 1948. It is now known as AK Steel. Like the North American steel industry in general, the size of the company has been greatly reduced from the 45,000 employees that it once had.

The Steamer ARMCO departed on its maiden voyage from Lorain, Ohio on June 6, 1953 in ballast for Superior, Wisconsin to load a cargo of iron ore. The carrier is shown in this photograph while passing downbound in the West Neebish Channel, St. Mary's River, on August 6, 1995.

Steamer BUCKEYE (3)

OWNER:	Oglebay Norton Company, Marine Transportation
BUILT:	Bethlehem Steel Corporation, Shipbuilding Division, Sparrows Point, Maryland - 1952
HULL NO.:	4505
O. A. DIMENSIONS:	698'6" x 70' x 37'
FORMER DATA:	Launched as the bulk freighter SPARROWS POINT. Lengthened 72' at American Ship Building Company, Chicago, Illinois in 1958. Converted to a self-unloader at Fraser Shipyards, Inc., Superior, Wisconsin in 1980. Given present name in 1991.

The Korean War demand created a shortfall of carrying capacity on the Great Lakes for all the increased quantities of iron ore that needed to be moved for the North American steel industry. All building berths on the lakes were booked, so Bethlehem Steel built this carrier for themselves from the keel to completion on the East Coast. The vessel was then towed up the Mississippi River System and entered Lake Michigan at Chicago, Illinois.

When Bethlehem decided to dispose of this vessel in 1990, Oglebay Norton was the successful bidder. The current name was selected at a board meeting on February 28th and returned a name that had been used in the fleet dating back over 45 years. The reference is to the State of Ohio, commonly known as "The Buckeye State."

The Steamer BUCKEYE (3) is shown in this photograph while passing downbound in the West Neebish Channel, St. Mary's River, on May 29, 1995.

Steamer COURTNEY BURTON

OWNER:	Oglebay Norton Company, Marine Transportation
BUILT:	American Ship Building Company, Lorain, Ohio - 1953
HULL NO.:	869
O. A. DIMENSIONS:	690' x 70' x 37'
FORMER DATA:	Launched as the bulk freighter ERNEST T. WEIR (2) Given present name in 1978. Converted to a self-unloader at Bay Shipbuilding Corporation, Sturgeon Bay, Wisconsin in 1981.

Mr. Courtney Burton was the grandson of the late Earl W. Oglebay and was associated with Oglebay Norton Company all of his adult life. He was born in Cleveland, Ohio on October 29, 1912 and attended the Michigan Institute of Technology before joining Oglebay as a director of E. W. Oglebay Company in 1934.

When several associated companies were merged to form Oglebay Norton Company in 1957, Mr. Burton was elected chairman of the board and chairman of the executive committee. He was active in numerous charitable organizations and on the boards of financial institutions and national organizations at the time of his death in Gates Mills, Ohio on August 19, 1992.

His namesake sailed on its maiden trip April 12, 1953 in ballast from Lorain, Ohio to Superior, Wisconsin to load iron ore. It is shown in this photograph while downbound in the West Neebish Channel, St. Mary's River, on June 24, 1996.

Motor Vessel COLUMBIA STAR

OWNER: Oglebay Norton Company, Marine Transportation
BUILT: Bay Shipbuilding Corporation,
Sturgeon Bay, Wisconsin - 1981
HULL NO.: 726
O. A. DIMENSIONS: 1,000' x 105' x 56'

The thousand-foot Motor Vessel COLUMBIA STAR was the first of that class in this fleet. Originally, it was dedicated primarily to moving iron ore pellets from Silver Bay, Minnesota to the TORCO Dock at Toledo, Ohio. When this fleet won a large percentage of the western coal float from Detroit Edison Company, this carrier, and a sistership which was added in 1990, began moving coal as well.

The first word of this ship's name honors the fleet which was formerly called Columbia Transportation/Division. In turn, Columbia referred to the Brig COLUMBIA which carried the first cargo of iron ore through the St. Mary's Falls Canal in 1855. The second word was in reference to the star which Oglebay Norton vessels formerly carried on their smoke stacks, but which have now been deleted in favor of the bow logo.

This carrier sailed on its maiden voyage in ballast from Sturgeon Bay, Wisconsin on May 30, 1981 to load iron ore pellets at Silver Bay, Minnesota for Lorain, Ohio delivery. It is shown while passing downbound in the West Neebish Channel, St. Mary's River, on May 29, 1995.

Motor Vessel JOSEPH H. FRANTZ

OWNER:	Oglebay Norton Company, Marine Transportation
BUILT:	Great Lakes Engineering Works, River Rouge, Michigan - 1925
HULL NO.:	248
O. A. DIMENSIONS:	618' x 62' x 32'
FORMER DATA:	Launched as a bulk freighter. Converted to a self-unloader at Christy Corporation, Sturgeon Bay, Wisconsin in 1965.

The namesake of this diesel-powered vessel is Mr. Joseph Henry Frantz. He was born January 24, 1864 in Cincinnati, Ohio and was educated in the public schools. He began his career in 1884 with the Cincinnati Corregation Company, then joined the Piqua Rolling Mill Company in 1889 as its secretary. From 1902 through 1917 he was vice president of the Columbus Iron and Steel Company.

Mr. Frantz became affiliated with the American Rolling Mill Company as vice president in 1917. He was elected its vice chairman in 1930 and chairman in 1937. He died at Columbus, Ohio on August 19, 1938.

The Motor Vessel JOSEPH H. FRANTZ is shown while inbound with limestone from Marblehead, Ohio on the Cuyahoga River at Cleveland, Ohio on August 2, 1995.

Steamer MIDDLETOWN

OWNER:	Oglebay Norton Company, Marine Transportation
BUILT:	Bethlehem Shipbuilding and Drydock Company, Sparrows Point, Maryland - 1943
HULL NO.:	4381
O. A. DIMENSIONS:	730' x 75' x 39'3"
FORMER DATA:	Launched as the tanker MARQUETTE. Renamed NESHANIC in 1943. Renamed GULFOIL in 1947. Rebuilt, lengthened 228'3", converted to a bulk freighter with new midbody and renamed PIONEER CHALLENGER at Maryland Shipbuilding Company, Baltimore, Maryland in 1961. Given present name in 1962. Converted to a self-unloader at Bay Shipbuilding Corporation, Sturgeon Bay, Wisconsin in 1982.

The Steamer MIDDLETOWN honors the home location of AK Steel, formerly known as Armco Steel, at Middletown, Ohio. It is located in Butler County and has a population of about 40,000. The community is on the east bank of the Miami River midway between Dayton and Cincinnati, whence comes its name.

The city was founded in 1802 and quickly became an agricultural center. In 1900 Mr. George M. Verity built a mill there that produced sheet steel by the continuous rolling process. This was the start of what became Armco Steel Corporation. Oglebay Norton Company has provided Armco's Great Lakes transportation needs for over sixty years.

The Steamer MIDDLETOWN is shown while downbound with iron ore in the West Neebish Channel, St. Mary's River, on August 4, 1995.

Motor Vessel DAVID Z. NORTON (3)

OWNER:	Oglebay Norton Company, Marine Transportation
BUILT:	American Ship Building Company, Lorain, Ohio - 1973
HULL NO.:	901
O. A. DIMENSIONS:	630' x 68' x 36'11"
FORMER DATA:	Launched as WILLIAM R. ROESCH. Given present name in 1995.

When this diesel-powered self-unloader entered service, it was named in honor of the chairman, president and chief executive officer of Jones & Laughlin Steel Corporation because the original owner built this carrier, and its sistership, on the basis of a new, long-term iron ore hauling contract with J & L.

In the restructuring process during 1993-1995 of this owner, many changes were made both to the "look" of their vessels and, in this case, to the name.

The DAVID Z. NORTON sailed on its maiden trip July 7, 1973 light to Superior, Wisconsin to load iron ore pellets. Its namesake was Mr. David Zadock Norton, born in Cleveland, Ohio on June 1, 1851. Following a banking career, he joined with Mr. Earl W.Oglebay in 1890 to form Oglebay Norton Company to engage in the iron ore merchant trade. He retired in 1919 and died in Cleveland on January 6, 1928.

The Motor Vessel DAVID Z. NORTON is shown in this photograph while inbound with iron ore pellets from Lorain, Ohio for LTV Steel on April 15, 1995. The scene is while passing through the Cuyahoga River at Cleveland, Ohio.

Motor Vessel OGLEBAY NORTON

OWNER:	Oglebay Norton Company, Marine Transportation
BUILT:	Bay Shipbuilding Corporation, Sturgeon Bay, Wisconsin - 1978
HULL NO.:	717
O. A. DIMENSIONS:	1,000' x 105' x 56'
FORMER DATA:	Launched as LEWIS WILSON FOY. Given present name in 1991.

The Motor Vessel OGLEBAY NORTON became the second "1,000'er" in this fleet with conclusion of its purchase late in December 1990 from Bethlehem Steel Corporation. The carrier was laid-up at Toledo, Ohio, then officially renamed at the board of directors meeting on February 28th to begin serving under its new name in 1991.

This vessel sailed on its maiden voyage from Sturgeon Bay, Wisconsin, in ballast, to Superior, Wisconsin on June 8, 1978 to take on a cargo of 57,952 gross tons of taconite pellets for delivery to Burns Harbor, Indiana.

Oglebay Norton Company itself is the namesake. Headquarters are located in downtown Cleveland, Ohio. The firm has been involved in shipping and iron ore mining for over a hundred years until it sold its interest in the Eveleth Mines properties at the end of 1996.

The Motor Vessel OGLEBAY NORTON is shown passing downbound in the West Neebish Channel, St. Mary's River, on May 30, 1995.

Motor Vessel EARL W. OGLEBAY

OWNER:	Oglebay Norton Company, Marine Transportation
BUILT:	American Ship Building Company, Lorain, Ohio - 1973
HULL NO.:	902
O. A. DIMENSIONS:	630' x 68' x 36'11"
FORMER DATA:	Launched as PAUL THAYER. Given present name in 1995.

This self-unloader departed Lorain, Ohio on its maiden voyage November 15, 1973, light for Escanaba, Michigan to load iron ore pellets for Cleveland, Ohio delivery. Its original namesake was the chairman of the board of Ling-Temco-Vought, Inc., then the parent company of Jones & Laughlin Steel Corporation. Like the NORTON (3), it was constructed to serve in the trade of that steel company.

The carrier's current namesake was Colonel Earl Wadsworth Oglebay. He was born April 16, 1840 in Wheeling, West Virginia. Following schooling, he became a prominent banker, then joined with David Zadock Norton in 1890 to form this owning company. The firm operated eleven iron ore mines in the Lake Superior District by the time Mr. Oglebay died in Cleveland, Ohio on June 22, 1926.

A former bulk freighter honored him during the period 1896 - 1930 in the Steamer E. W. OGLEBAY. This motor vessel is shown above while outbound in the Cuyahoga River at Cleveland, Ohio on its first trip under this name. The date was April 1, 1995 and the vessel was then running four consecutive shuttle runs from Lorain, Ohio to Cleveland for LTV Steel.

Steamer RESERVE

OWNER:	Oglebay Norton Company, Marine Transportation
BUILT:	Great Lakes Engineering Works, River Rouge, Michigan - 1953
HULL NO.:	299
O. A. DIMENSIONS:	767' x 70' x 36'
FORMER DATA:	Launched as a bulk freighter. Lengthened 120' at Fraser Shipyards, Inc., Superior, Wisconsin in 1975. Converted to a self-unloader at Bay Shipbuilding Corporation, Sturgeon Bay, Wisconsin in 1983.

The Steamer RESERVE took its name from Reserve Mining Company. It was a company jointly owned by Armco and Republic Steel Corporations when formed in 1950. After Republic and Jones & Laughlin merged to become LTV Steel, and the company went bankrupt in July 1986, Reserve Mining shut its doors.

The Reserve Mining iron ore pellet plant is located at Silver Bay, Minnesota on the north shore of Lake Superior. After it had been shuttered for a few years, the property was taken over by Cleveland-Cliffs Iron Company under the name of Northshore Mining Company. Annual rated capacity is 4 million gross tons of taconite pellets.

This carrier cleared Detroit, Michigan on April 27, 1953 on its maiden voyage. It was upbound in ballast to Superior, Wisconsin to load iron ore. The Steamer RESERVE is shown passing downbound in the West Neebish Channel, St. Mary's River, on May 29, 1995.

Motor Vessel FRED R. WHITE, JR.

OWNER:	Oglebay Norton Company, Marine Transportation
BUILT:	Bay Shipbuilding Corporation, Sturgeon Bay, Wisconsin - 1979
HULL NO.:	722
O. A. DIMENSIONS:	636'6" x 68' x 40'

The Motor Vessel FRED R. WHITE, JR. sailed on its maiden voyage in ballast from Sturgeon Bay, Wisconsin to Escanaba, Michigan to load iron ore pellets on May 26, 1979. The cargo was delivered to Cleveland, Ohio. The carrier is shown while downbound in the West Neebish Channel, St. Mary's River, on May 29, 1995.

Mr. Fred Rollin White, Jr. was the carrier's namesake. He was born in Cleveland, Ohio on March 23, 1913 and graduated from Yale Univeristy with a B.A. degree in 1935. Thereupon, he joined Oglebay Norton as an accountant in the vessel operations of Columbia Transportation Company. He progressed upwards and in 1949, was elected a vice president and director of the firm.

In 1960, Mr. White became senior vice president - transportation and docks and also served as treasurer in the 1960-1963 period. In 1969 he was elected vice chairman of the board of Oglebay Norton.

From October 1, 1978 onward, he served as chairman of the company's executive committee and a director. Mr White died in Cleveland on December 10, 1995.

Motor Vessel WOLVERINE (4)

OWNER:	Oglebay Norton Company, Marine Transportation
BUILT:	American Ship Building Company, Lorain, Ohio - 1974
HULL NO.:	903
O. A. DIMENSIONS:	630' x 68' x 36'11"

This motor vessel began service on October 15, 1974 when it departed Lorain, Ohio in ballast bound for Stoneport, Michigan to take on a cargo of limestone for Huron, Ohio delivery. It is shown in this photograph while outbound on the Cuyahoga River in Cleveland, Ohio on April 20, 1995.

Fleet managers brought back this name from that of a bulk freighter in their fleet which had been retired in 1954 and scrapped in 1971. Wolverine is the mascot of the State of Michigan. It seemed appropriate to use the name again since so much of the fleet's commerce was to and from Michigan ports.

The wolverine is the largest of American fur-bearing animals of the family Mustelidae. The animal was formerly found in abundance in Michigan and the Great Lakes region, but today it is mostly found in the Rocky Mountains and northward as far as the Arctic.

Motor Vessel WOLFE ISLANDER III

OWNER:	Ontario Ministry of Transportation & Communication
BUILT:	Port Arthur Shipbuilding Company, Thunder Bay, Ontario - 1975
HULL NO.:	128
O. A. DIMENSIONS:	205′ x 65′ x 11′6″

The Motor Vessel WOLFE ISLANDER III has an automobile carrying capacity of 50 cars and can also accommodate 338 persons. It was built to replace a smaller combination package freight-carferry vessel on the run between Wolfe Island and Kingston, Ontario. The older vessel was simply called WOLFE ISLANDER.

The namesake of this modern carferry is Wolfe Island, Ontario. This is a large island at the entrance to the St. Lawrence River, opposite the city of Kingston, Ontario and at the northeast extremity of Lake Ontario. It forms a township of Frontenac County and divides the St. Lawrence River into two navigable branches; the main one, on the United States side is also the boundary between the two countries.

Wolfe Island has a number of picturesque bays and beaches, making it a popular summer resort. It is 21 miles long and 7 miles at its greatest width. Its area of 31,319 acres consists mainly of excellent farming land, and extensive cultivation has taken place. At one time it was known as Grande Isle and was a part of La Salle's seigniory. Governor Simcoe renamed it in 1792 in honor of the victor at Quebec in that year. The vessel is shown above departing its dock at Kingston, Ontario, bound for Wolfe Island, on October 3, 1981.

Motor Vessel CHI-CHEEMAUN

OWNER:	Ontario Northland Transportation Commission
BUILT:	Collingwood Shipyards, Collingwood, Ontario—1974
HULL NO.:	205
O. A. DIMENSIONS:	365′5″ × 61′ × 21′

This modern passenger and automobile ferry was built under a plan by the government of the Province of Ontario whereby they would provide modern, swift ferry service from the tip of the Bruce County peninsula of that province to Manitoulin Island, also in Ontario. Specifically, service was designed to serve Tobermory, Ontario on the mainland and South Bay Mouth on Manitoulin Island. For a number of years ferries operated privately by this firm served on this trade route, however, with traffic increasing and demands for new tonnage the Ontario government stepped in to supply needed funds for this vessel.

This vessel has a capacity of one hundred-thirteen automobiles and five hundred-thirty passengers, contrasted to smaller vessels hitherto used on the route of about half the capacity or less. The Motor Vessel CHI-CHEEMAUN is powered by a 7,000 shaft horsepower diesel engine and is capable of speeds of 20 miles per hour or greater.

The name for this vessel was chosen by committee, it being made up of local citizens of Manitoulin Island and the area of the Bruce County peninsula. *CHI-CHEEMAUN* is a name from the Ojibway Indian language meaning, literally, "the big canoe." Since this is the largest ferry ever operated in this service it is a most appropriate namesake. The ship is shown above on arrival at Tobermory, Ontario on May 18, 1980.

Motor Vessel NINDAWAYMA

OWNER: Ontario Northland Transportation Commission
BUILT: S. A. Juliana Constructora Gijonsea, Gijon, Spain - 1976
HULL NO.: 243
O. A. DIMENSIONS: 333'6" x 55' x 36'6"
FORMER DATA: Launched as MONTE CRUCETA. Renamed MONTE CASTILLO in 1976. Renamed MANX VIKING in 1978. Renamed MANX in 1987. Renamed SKUDENES in 1987. Renamed ONTARIO NO. 1 (2) in 1989. Given present name in 1989.

The ferry Motor Vessel NINDAWAYMA went into service for this owner on June 29, 1989. Its last previous name was given in January, 1989 for the purpose of crossing the Atlantic Ocean and getting into the Great Lakes. A contest was sponsored by the owner in the spring of 1989 for a new name for the ferry's service between the ports of South Baymouth, on Manitoulin Island, and Tobermory, at the northern end of the Bruce Peninsula.

The "winning" name was suggested by a lady from Owen Sound, Ontario. It is from the Ojibway Indian language and, roughly translated, means "little sister." The name refers to the fact that this vessel is somewhat smaller than the other vessel on the run, the Motor Vessel CHI-CHEEMAUN.

It should be noted for historians that the name MANX was only on the ship about two weeks, for its trip from England to Norway in 1987. The vessel has a carrying capacity of 130 automobiles and 400 passengers. It is shown while underway in August, 1989.

Motor Vessel EMMET J. CAREY

OWNER:	Osborne Materials Company
BUILT:	Hugh E. Lee Iron Works, Saginaw, Michigan - 1948
HULL NO.:	None assigned.
O. A. DIMENSIONS:	114' x 23' x 11'
FORMER DATA:	Launched as BEATRICE OTTINGER. Lengthened 50' and renamed JAMES B. LYONS at American Ship Building Company, Lorain, Ohio in 1963. Given present name in 1988.

This vessel operated out of the port of Lorain, Ohio from the time of its construction until being sold in late 1989 to this owner.

The Motor Vessel EMMET J. CAREY is a sandsucker which is utilized to dredge from the bottom of Lake Erie. It is shown in this photograph while at its berth in Erie, Pennsylvania on September 23, 1988.

Namesake of this carrier is Mr. Emmet John Carey who was born in Erie, Pennsylvania on July 24, 1924. He was locally educated and attended Gannon College before entering the business world. In 1949 he joined Erie Builders as assistant manager. He was named president in 1962, upon the death of his father-in-law, and retired from that position in 1983. Mr. Carey now lives mainly in Florida but assists his son in the firm during the summer months. His hobbies are golf and "watching football," according to his wife.

Motor Vessel F. M. OSBORNE (2)

OWNER:	Osborne Materials Company
BUILT:	J. Butman & T. Horn, Buffalo, New York - 1910
HULL NO.:	None assigned
O. A. DIMENSIONS:	150′ x 29′ x 11′3″
FORMER DATA:	Launched as the carferry GRAND ISLAND (1). Converted to a sandsucker at Lorain Elyria Sand Company, Lorain, Ohio in 1954. Lengthened 40′ at L. A. Wells Construction Company, Cleveland, Ohio and renamed LESCO in 1958. Given present name in 1975.

The Motor Vessel F.M. OSBORNE (2) is named for Mr. Frank Marion Osborne who was born March 12, 1855 in Girard, Ohio. He was educated in the public schools and began work in the steel mills. In 1873 he went to Cleveland to take a job as a bookkeeper with Card & Company, coal brokers. In 1880 he formed his own coal firm known as Osborne, Saeger & Company. This firm acquired various coal properties through the years and brought them into production. In 1899 he merged these interests into Pittsburg Coal Company and became its president.

Mr. Osborne served in this capacity until 1902 when he formed Youghiogheny & Ohio Coal Company and became its president. He continued in this capacity until his death at Toledo, Ohio on July 15, 1911. This firm was a major coal shipper on the Great Lakes and the former Steamer MUNISING bore his name in 1903 when it was commissioned. His grandson, Mr. Jerome Osborne, now president of this owning firm, thought it fitting to honor his grandfather with the naming of this vessel.

It is shown above at Grand River, Ohio on October 29, 1976.

Steamer MAPLEGLEN (2)

OWNER:	P. & H. Shipping Division, Parrish & Heimbecker Limited
BUILT:	Collingwood Shipyards, Collingwood, Ontario - 1960
HULL NO.:	165
O. A. DIMENSIONS:	715'3" x 75' x 37'9"
FORMER DATA:	Launched as CAROL LAKE. Renamed ALGOCAPE (1) in 1987. Given present name in 1994.

The namesake of this modern bulk freighter was chosen with the common fleet suffix "glen," in mind and without knowledge that there was actually prior use of the name in Canadian registry. MAPLEGLEN (1) was a wooden, small bulk freighter owned by Canada Steamship Lines in the period 1920-1925, before its being scuttled in Lake Ontario.

The maple tree, long a symbol of Canada, was the actual namesake reference. Maple trees are common not only in Canada, but in almost all of North America. They are reknowned for their colorful leaves during the fall months of the year.

Shortly after the modern St. Lawrence Seaway opened, this vessel was one of the first to operate in the waterway to full capacity. It had been sought by this owner for several years and, finally, was acquired following the sale of vessels in GLBC, Inc. to Algoma Central Marine and ULS Corporation in the spring of 1994. The carrier is shown in this photograph while downbound in the West Neebish Channel, St. Mary's River, on July 14, 1994.

Steamer OAKGLEN (2)

OWNER: P. & H. Shipping Division, Parrish & Heimbecker Limited
BUILT: Midland Shipyards,
Midland, Ontario - 1954
HULL NO.: 37
O. A. DIMENSIONS: 714'6" x 70'3" x 37'3"
FORMER DATA: Launched as T. R. McLAGAN. Given present name in 1990.

The bulk freight Steamer OAKGLEN (2) was the last vessel to be constructed at this shipyard. Following christening ceremonies, a routine shut-down of the facility began, and all further vessel construction in Georgian Bay took place at Collingwood, Ontario.

The first time this ship name was used on the Great Lakes was in 1982 when these owners purchased the vessel assets of the defunct Soo River Company. The vessel formerly bearing this name was sold for scrap in 1988.

The Steamer OAKGLEN (2) is the largest vessel to be operated by this company, and is its flagship. The namesake reference was to the OAK tree, specifically, because of its hardy nature and long life. The common suffix, GLEN, was also utilized.

This modern Great Lakes carrier is shown in this photograph passing downbound in the West Neebish Channel, St. Mary's River, on July 17, 1990.

This vessel sailed on its maiden voyage to Superior Wisconsin, arriving there April 25, 1954, to load 18,609 gross tons of iron ore for delivery to Hamilton Ontario.

Motor Vessel CARTIERDOC (2)

OWNER:	N. M. Paterson & Sons Limited
BUILT:	Schlieker-Werft, Hamburg, West Germany - 1959
HULL NO.:	535-Schlieker-Werft and 693-Davie
O. A. DIMENSIONS:	730' x 75'9" x 40'2"
FORMER DATA:	Launched as EMS ORE. Renamed MONTCLIFFE HALL in 1976. Lengthened 184' and widened 1'8" with new forebody at Davie Shipbuilding Limited, Lauzon, Quebec in 1977. Given present name in 1988.

The modern Motor Vessel CARTIERDOC (2) honors Jacques Cartier, navigator and discoverer of the St. Lawrence River valley in 1534-35.

He was born August 15, 1491 in St. Malo, France and sailed his ship, commissioned by Frances I, into the Gulf of St. Lawrence in 1534 via the Strait of Belle Isle. Cartier had been on a mission to find a northwest passage to the Spice Islands, and landed in the St. Lawrence.

He returned in 1535 in search of the fabled mines of the Saguenay Indians. Further details of Cartier's adventures in Canada and those of his associates make interesting reading, but are to lenghthy to be told here.

Cartier's namesake bulk freighter is shown in this photograph in the St. Mary's River, near Sault Ste. Marie, Michigan, on July 18, 1988.

Motor Vessel COMEAUDOC

OWNER:	N. M. Paterson & Sons Limited
BUILT:	Collingwood Shipyards, Collingwood, Ontario—1960
HULL NO.:	164
O. A. DIMENSIONS:	730′ × 75′6″ × 37′9″
FORMER DATA:	Launched as MURRAY BAY (2). Given present name in 1963.

With the familiar "doc", meaning Dominion of Canada in the N. M. Paterson & Sons fleet, this vessel takes its name from Baie Comeau, Quebec, a frequent port of call for the carrier. Baie Comeau is a city of about 11,000 population located about one and one-half miles north of the mouth of the Manicouagan River on the north shore of the St. Lawrence River.

The area was developed largely by the Quebec North Shore Paper Company Limited who began a pulpwood mill there in the 1930's. Today it not only serves that industry but also the large Canadian British Aluminium Company Limited and Cargill Grain Company Limited. It is the latter relationship which brought about the selection of this name for this carrier. The Patersons and Cargill have had a close business relationship for some years and when that firm built the first large export grain elevator at Baie Comeau, the fleet was a frequent caller.

The port of Baie Comeau has about 8,500,000 net tons of commerce annually and the 13,898,000 bushel capacity grain elevator is a major contributor to that tonnage. The vessel sailed on its maiden trip April 9, 1960 from Collingwood, Ontario to Fort William, Ontario to load grain. It is shown while downbound with grain in the West Neebish Channel, St. Mary's River on August 12, 1986, not long after it entered service with a diesel power plant.

Motor Vessel MANTADOC (2)

OWNER:	N. M. Paterson & Sons Limited
BUILT:	Collingwood Shipyards, Collingwood, Ontario—1967
HULL NO.:	187
O. A. DIMENSIONS:	607′9″ × 62′ × 36′

The Province of Manitoba in central Canada is the namesake of this ship. This fleet has a policy of ending most of their ship names with "doc", meaning Dominion of Canada. Prominent places in its operations and provinces in Canada provide a wide assortment of names for their ships.

The Province of Manitoba has an area of approximately 251,000 square miles and a population of about 900,000. The main focal point of the province is the city of Winnipeg, located in the southeastern part of its area. Winnipeg is the largest city in the province and is a main transportation hub. The Winnipeg Grain Exchange is also located there and is the headquarters for grain trading in Canada. Many fleet operators have wholly-owned subsidiary firms as members of the Exchange, providing a convenient arrangement for shippers and carriers to fulfill their common interests of moving grain on the Great Lakes.

The owners of the Motor Vessel MANTADOC are prominent grain elevator operators in Canada and many of their operations are in this province. It is fitting, then, that this vessel should be called Motor Vessel MANTADOC. The ship is shown upbound in the Welland Ship Canal on April 26, 1988.

Motor Vessel PATERSON (2)

OWNER:	N. M. Paterson & Sons Limited
BUILT:	Collingwood Shipyards, Collingwood, Ontario - 1985
HULL NO.:	231
O. A. DIMENSIONS:	736'6" x 75'10" x 42'

The bulk freight Motor Vessel PATERSON (2) began life when the keel was laid November 5, 1984. It was launched on April 18, 1985 and sailed on its maiden voyage June 27, 1985, light from Collingwood to Thunder Bay, Ontario to load a cargo of grain for Quebec City, Quebec delivery.

This carrier incorporates many features enabling it to deal with early winter season weather operations on the Great Lakes. The exended ram bow is ideally suited to provide ice breaking capabilities, and modern, fuel efficient engines provide 8,160 shaft horsepower. Carrying capacity is 28,500 gross tons at Seaway draft and 32,800 gross tons at the ship's full loadline draft.

This vessel name honors the entire Paterson family. The late Senator Norman M. Paterson founded the firm and younger members of the family still operate and manage the affairs of this private company at headquarters in Thunder Bay, Ontario.

The Motor Vessel PATERSON (2) is shown passing downbound in the West Neebish Channel, St. Mary's River with a cargo of grain on August 15, 1986.

Motor Vessel QUEDOC (3)

OWNER:	N. M. Paterson & Sons Limited
BUILT:	Davie Shipbuilding, Limited Lauzon, Quebec - 1965
HULL NO.:	655
O. A. DIMENSIONS:	730' x 75' x 39'2"
FORMER DATA:	Launched as BEAVERCLIFFE HALL. Given present name in 1988.

While operating under its former name, this motor vessel established a Great Lakes cargo record on July 27, 1967 when it lifted 987,010 bushels of corn at South Chicago, Illinois for delivery to Quebec City, Quebec. The record stood until broken by another lake carrier on September 17, 1969.

The Motor Vessel QUEDOC (3) carries on a proud name of ships in the Paterson Fleet. The first steamer to bear this name was built in 1890 and was named QUEDOC (1) in 1926. All of the vessels named QUEDOC were named in honor of the province of Quebec, Dominion of Canada.

Quebec is the largest French-speaking province of Canada and Montreal, Quebec is the second largest French-speaking city in the world, next to Paris, France.

The Motor Vessel QUEDOC (3) is shown in this photograph winding in the Kaministiquia River at Thunder Bay, Ontario on July 11, 1990.

Motor Vessel VANDOC (2)

OWNER: N. M. Paterson & Sons Limited
BUILT: Collingwood Shipyards, Collingwood, Ontario - 1964
HULL NO.: 179
O. A. DIMENSIONS: 605′ x 62′ x 33′10″
FORMER DATA: Launched as SIR DENYS LOWSON. Given present name in 1979.

The Motor Vessel VANDOC (2) is a bulk freighter in marked contrast to the first ship in this fleet to bear this name. This vessel is diesel-powered and twice the carrier, in terms of capacity, compared to the first VANDOC which was built in 1898, was coal-fired and carried about 7,000 gross tons.

This vessel takes the city of Vancouver, British Columbia as its namesake, with the usual fleet suffix, doc, added to the ship name. Vancouver is the largest city and most important seaport of Canada on the Pacific Coast. It is located at the mouth of the Fraser River delta and has a population of about 550,000.

Vancouver took its name from Captain George Vancouver of the Royal Navy who explored the area in 1792. Growth really began when the Canadian Pacific Railway was completed to the site in the 1880's. It was incorporated as a city in 1886. The city lies in a beautiful mountain setting and is known for its moderate climate.

This vessel is shown below while upbound in Lake Nicolet, St. Mary's River on June 12, 1980.

Motor Vessel WINDOC (2)

OWNER:	N. M. Paterson & Sons Limited
BUILT:	Schlieker-Werft, Hamburg, West Germany - 1959
HULL NO.:	533-Schlieker-Werft; 694-Davie
O. A. DIMENSIONS:	730' x 75'9" x 40'2"
FORMER DATA:	Launched as RHINE ORE. Renamed STEELCLIFFE HALL in 1976. Lengthened 184' and widened 1'8" with new forebody at Davie Shipbuilding Limited, Lauzon, Quebec in 1978. Given present name in 1988.

The Motor Vessel WINDOC (2) takes its name in reference to the city of Winnipeg, Manitoba. Winnipeg is the grain trading and merchandising capital of the Western world. All of the international grain trading companies have an office or a representative on the Winnipeg Grain Exchange. This vessel owner is one of those firms. Paterson has a chartering broker in Winnipeg as well as its grain merchandising headquarters.

Winnipeg is the fourth largest city in Canada with a current population of about 350,000. The city's name comes from the Cree Indians. That tribe has words "win," and "nipee," which mean, together, muddy water.

The Motor Vessel WINDOC (2) is shown in this photograph passing upbound at Port Colborne, Ontario, in the Welland Ship Canal, on April 30, 1997.

Motor Vessel JIIMAAN

OWNER:	Pelee Island Transportation Services
BUILT:	Port Weller Dry Docks, St. Catharines, Ontario - 1992
HULL NO.:	76
O. A. DIMENSIONS:	200' x 48' x 15'

The modern Motor Vessel JIIMAAN is a combination passenger and automobile carferry which operates between the United States port of Sandusky, Ohio, Pelee Island and the Canadian ports of Leamington or Kingsville, Ontario. It has a capacity for forty normal-sized automobiles and is licensed to transport four hundred passengers. The carrier is powered by two diesel engines which develop 2,800 brake horsepower in total.

The name chosen for this carferry was selected in a contest conducted among grade school students living on Pelee Island, Canada. Their teachers were the ultimate decision makers in selecting the name. It is a name native to the Ojibway Indians and, loosely translated, means "little Canoe."

Entering service in early summer of 1992, the vessel now provides much-needed carrying capacity in the fleet in the transport of people between the points named above. The route has become not only a pleasant short-cut between northern Ohio and southwestern Ontario, but a relaxing one which is gaining popularity with local residents.

The Motor Vessel JIIMAAN is shown in this photograph while underway on Lake Erie in 1992 shortly after being commissioned.

Barge PERE MARQUETTE 41

OWNER:	Pere Marquette Shipping Company
BUILT:	Manitowoc Shipbuilding Company, Manitowoc, Wisconsin - 1941
HULL NO.:	311
O. A. DIMENSIONS:	403' x 58' x 23'6"
FORMER DATA:	Launched as the powered carferry steamer CITY OF MIDLAND 41. Shortened 4', converted to a crane-equipped bulk freight barge and given present name at Bay Shipbuilding Corporation, Sturgeon Bay, Wisconsin in 1998.

Following the above conversion, the numeral "41" was kept in this barge's name for historical reference to its original name. The name PERE MARQUETTE portion of the name refers to the original owning company - the Pere Marquette Railway. The French missionary Father Marquette was the namesake reference.

This carrier made its maiden voyage on March 12, 1941 when it sailed from Manitowoc, Wisconsin to Ludington, Michigan with passengers and freight cars.

Two 25-ton material handling cranes are on deck which can use hooks, buckets or magnets for cargo movements. The Barge PERE MARQUETTE 41 is shown proceeding upbound, with the Tug DAUNTLESS on the stern, with a diesel generator cargo from Ogdensburg, New York bound for Burns Harbor, Indiana on November 21, 1998.

Motor Vessel HAMILTON ENERGY

OWNER:	Provmar Fuels, Inc.
BUILT:	Grangemouth Dockyard Company, Limited, Grangemouth, Scotland - 1965
HULL NO.:	535
O. A. DIMENSIONS:	201'6" x 34'1" x 14'7"
FORMER DATA:	Launched as PARTINGTON. Renamed SHELL SCIENTIST in 1979. Renamed METRO SUN in 1981. Given present name in 1985.

The diminutive tank Motor Vessel HAMILTON ENERGY was put into service in Hamilton, Ontario harbor in mid-1985 by this firm to answer a joint need for local bunkering service of ULS Corporation and Canada Steamship Lines, both of which had large activity in Hamilton in the delivery of iron ore pellets, coal and limestone.

Prior to the advent of this service, a bunkering barge of Shell Canada, Limited provided such service. Upon relocation of that barge, however, the need for an alternative existed, and this vessel was acquired to fill the void.

In addition to this unit's mobility the former Motor Vessel UNGAVA TRANSPORT and Steamer IMPERIAL SARNIA were acquired, their engines removed and the hulls permanently moored at Hamilton to serve as off-load "mother ships" to this vessel.

Simply, the namesake reference is to the fact this vessel is based in Hamilton and that it provides ENERGY (oil) to these fleets and any others which require it. The vessel is shown enroute to bunker a vessel in Hamilton harbor on July 16, 1986.

Barge CHIEF WAWATAM

OWNER:	Purvis Marine Limited
BUILT:	Toledo Shipbuilding Company, Toledo, Ohio - 1911
HULL NO.:	119
O. A. DIMENSIONS:	347' x 62'3" x 15'
FORMER DATA:	Launched as a powered railroad carferry. Converted to a bulk freight barge and shortened 4' at Purvis Marine Limited, Sault Ste. Marie, Ontario in 1989.

The venerable hull of the original carferry lives on in this steel-hulled bulk freight barge. Fortunately, the name lives on as well. This is so because the name of this Indian chief was famous from early days in the region of the Straits of Mackinac and the Soo.

The CHIEF WAWATAM sailed on its maiden voyage from Toledo on October 15, 1911. It went into service crossing the Straits immediately upon arrival and performed yeoman service on that route, both as a carferry and as an icebreaker for Great Lakes fleets, until the early 1980's when its condition prevented much use.

Chief Wawatam was of the Chippewa tribe and is said to have befriended Mr. Alexander Henry when he was a prisoner of the Chippewas by adopting him as a blood brother in 1763.

The Barge CHIEF WAWATAM is shown in the above photograph while passing downbound with a load of steel in the St. Mary's River in July, 1990. The tug pushing is ANGLIAN LADY.

Barge CHARLES W. JOHNSON

OWNER:	Purvis Marine Limited
BUILT:	Collingwood Shipbuilding Company Limited, Collingwood, Ontario - 1916
HULL NO.:	46
O. A. DIMENSIONS:	245' x 43'3" x 18'
FORMER DATA:	Launched as the tanker IOCOLITE. Renamed IMPERIAL KINGSTON in 1947. Converted to a dry cargo barge, shortened 13' and given present name at A. B. Mclean & Sons Limited, Sault Ste. Marie, Ontario in 1961.

The 1,700-ton capacity Barge CHARLES W. JOHNSON is shown while under tow in the St. Mary's River. The crane on deck was added at the time of conversion in 1961 and is a 5-ton capacity crawler crane. The vessel is used primarily for the movement of sand taken from the lake bed above the Soo Locks, but it also has been handy in the lightering of stranded vessels in the St. Mary's River system over the years.

Namesake of this carrier was Mr. Charles William Johnson who was born April 2, 1908 in Batter & Dunnett Township, Ontario. After high school, he worked at various jobs in the area, then saw opportunities in the field of marine construction and towing.

He joined A. B. McLean & Sons in 1929 and was promoted to marine superintendent in 1933. He later became the firm's general superintendent. Mr. Johnson oversaw conversion of this vessel. He died as a result of an accident on his namesake on June 23, 1964.

Barge MALDEN

OWNER:	Purvis Marine Limited
BUILT:	Russell Brothers Limited, Owen Sound, Ontario - 1946
HULL NO.:	568
O. A. DIMENSIONS:	150' x 41'9" x 10'3"

The dry cargo crane-equipped bulk freight Barge MALDEN was originally constructed for McQueen Marine Limited. The firm is now out of existance, but then was located at Amherstburg, Ontario. When choosing a name for this barge, the owner took a name that was important to its home base of operations.

Fort Malden is commemorated in Amherstburg by the Fort Malden National Historic Park which was so designated by the present site of the town of Amherstburg and was used as a defense post, having been erected between 1797 and 1799. It served as the British base in the War of 1812 and for Brock's attacks on the city of Detroit, Michigan.

The fort also played a part in history in 1838 when its garrison and the local militia repelled four attempts of the "Patriot" filibusters to invade Canada on the Detroit River frontier. Two museum buildings now stand on the site. In them are Indian, military, pioneer and Great Lakes materials. In 1851, the municipality of Amherstburg was separated from the township of Malden as a village with town powers.

Barge P. M. L. SALVAGER

OWNER:	Purvis Marine Limited
BUILT:	Marine Industries, Limited, Sorel, Quebec - 1945
HULL NO.:	148
O. A. DIMENSIONS:	341' x 54' x 27'
FORMER DATA:	Launched as an unnamed Landing Ship, Tank vessel. Converted to a bulk freight barge at Marine Industries, Limited, Sorel, Quebec and named BALSAM-BRANCH in 1955. Renamed M. I. L. BALSAM in 1973. Renamed TECHNO-BALSAM in 1977. Converted to a crane-equipped bulk freight barge at Port Arthur Shipbuilding Company, Thunder Bay, Ontario and renamed D. D. S. SALVAGER in 1977. Given present name in 1988.

The Barge P. M. L. SALVAGER, under its former owner, was intended to be used as a cement barge after its purchase by St. Lawrence Cement Company in 1981. This was for Lake Superior service. As events unfolded, the barge was never used for transport, and, after nearly 7 years of idleness at Duluth, Minnesota, it was sold to this owner.

The most recent former name was given the vessel by another former owner, Deep Diving Services of Thunder Bay, Ontario. The namesake reference in this case is to the P. M. and L. in this owner's corporate title.

The vessel is shown here while enroute to a salvage assignment on the Steamer BLACK BAY on August 11, 1989 in the St. Mary's River.

Motor Vessel YANKCANUCK (2)

OWNER: Purvis Marine Limited

BUILT: Collingwood Shipyards, Collingwood, Ontario - 1963

HULL NO.: 178

O. A. DIMENSIONS: 324'3" x 49' x 26'

FORMER DATA: Launched as a powered crane vessel. Converted to a crane-equipped barge at Purvis Marine Limited, Sault Ste. Marie, Ontario in 1991. Reconverted to a powered crane vessel at Purvis Marine Limited, Sault Ste. Marie, Ontario in 1993.

This carrier takes its name from the fact that its original manager, Captain Filicano (Frank) Manzzutti is a Canadian citizen and his wife is an American citizen. The prefix "YANK" is a term of unknown origin and is short for Yankee. The suffix "CANUCK" is a nickname sometimes used for Canadian persons. It can also be used as a noun.

The vessel was managed by Captain Manzzutti for Algoma Steel Corporation until they took over management themselves. When very difficult times hit them in 1990-1991, the vessel was sold to this owner to raise much-needed cash. Labor disagreements caused the carrier to be towed as a barge in the years shown above. These were reconciled in 1993.

The Motor Vessel YANKCANUCK is a very versatile ship and has been steadily trading into various ports unknown to it before being acquired by Purvis Marine. It is shown in the St. Mary's River on August 5, 1995.

Motor Vessel HORIZON MONTREAL

OWNER:	Shell Canada Products Limited
BUILT:	Collingwood Shipyards, Collingwood, Ontario - 1958
HULL NO.:	167
O. A. DIMENSIONS:	317'6" x 45'6" x 24'6"
FORMER DATA:	Launched as TYEE SHELL. Lengthened 68'6", widened 6', deepened 4'6" and renamed ARCTIC TRADER at Collingwood Shipyards, Collingwood, Ontario in 1969. Renamed RIVERSHELL (4) in 1983. Given present name in 1995.

The primary service of this tank vessel is performing bunkering in and around the port of Montreal, Quebec. The carrier has a capacity of 5,228 cubic meters of fuel oil and is a familiar sight to ships when visiting the Montreal area.

This tanker was rebuilt and enlarged in 1969 for service during the summer and fall months in the Arctic region of Canada. While it returned to serve in its present capacity, it is still classed for Arctic service should that need arise.

The name was changed in 1995 to honor the Port of MONTREAL and to recognize its beautiful HORIZON when viewed from the St. Lawrence River in almost any direction. The name also has a mellifluous sound according to Mr. Gilles Poirier, local manager of the vessel.

The Motor Vessel HORIZON MONTREAL is shown while berthed at its normal location in Montreal, Quebec Harbor on September 22, 1996.

Motor Vessel GEORGE A. STINSON

OWNER:	Stinson, Inc.
BUILT:	American Ship Building Company, Lorain, Ohio - 1978
HULL NO.:	907
O. A. DIMENSIONS:	1004' x 105' x 50'

The Motor Vessel GEORGE A. STINSON became the only "1,000-footer" in the National Steel Fleet when it went into service late in 1978. At christening ceremonies August 21, 1978 in Detroit, Michigan, the vessel was proclaimed by its namesake to be dedicated to the city of Detroit and those people and industry that supported the firm's Great Lakes Steel Division on Zug Island.

Mr. George Arthur Stinson was born in Camden, Arkansas on February 11, 1915 and received a B.A. degree from Northwestern University in 1936 and a J.D. degree in 1939 from Columbia University. Following admission to the Bar, he served as legal assistant in the Tax Force, Mr. Stinson joined the law firm of Cleary, Gottlieb, Friendly and Hamilton, serving there until 1961 when he joined National Steel as vice president and secretary.

He was elected a director of National in 1963, president in December of that year and chief executive in 1966. In May 1972, he was named chairman of the board. His namesake sailed on its maiden trip October 14, 1978 in ballast to Superior, Wisconsin to load iron ore pellets for Zug Island. It is shown passing downbound in the West Neebish Channel, St. Mary's River, on July 22, 1998.

Barge McKEE SONS

OWNER:	Upper Lakes Barge Lines, Inc.
BUILT:	Sun Shipbuilding and Drydock Company, Chester, Pennsylvania - 1945
HULL NO.:	354
O. A. DIMENSIONS:	579'2" x 71'6" x 38'6"
FORMER DATA:	Launched as the C-4 type carrier MARINE ANGEL. Rebuilt, lengthened 123', converted to a self-unloader at Maryland Drydock Company, Baltimore, Maryland in 1952 and at Manitowoc Shipbuilding, Incorporated, Manitowoc, Wisconsin in 1953. Given present name in 1953. Shortened 53'10" and converted to a self-unloading bulk freight barge by Upper Lakes Towing Company, Menominee, Michigan in 1992.

Three principals of Sand Products Corporation, Detroit, Michigan settled upon this name in 1953 in honor of their eleven sons. The men were born in Cedar County, Iowa as follows: Mark - 1887, Max - 1891 and Paul - 1893. The sons of these McKee brothers were named Miles, Hugh, Mark, Malcolm, Muir, Julian, Terry, Robert, Bradshaw, Brent and Paul.

The McKEE SONS was the first saltwater vessel to sail the Great Lakes as a self-unloader in modern times. The carrier is shown in this photograph while inbound with iron ore at Cleveland, Ohio on August 3, 1994.

Motor Vessel CANADIAN CENTURY

OWNER:	Upper Lakes Group, Inc.
BUILT:	Port Weller Dry Docks, St. Catharines, Ontario - 1967
HULL NO.:	41
O. A. DIMENSIONS:	730' x 75' x 45'

The Motor Vessel CANADIAN CENTURY set a new Great Lakes coal cargo record on December 8, 1967 by lifting 28,283 net tons at Conneaut, Ohio for delivery to the DOFASCO steel facility in Hamilton, Ontario. This record stood until September 2nd of the following year when it was broken by another ship in the fleet.

The self-unloader is shown in a very rare appearance while loading grain at Harvest States No. 2 Elevator in Superior, Wisconsin on July 8, 1987.

This carrier was commissioned in the Dominion of Canada's centennial year. This owner felt it appropriate to name the vessel in honor of Canada's CENTURY of confederation. As with many other vessels in this fleet, the word CANADIAN was used as the ship's first name word.

While 1967 was a year of celebration and commemoration throughout Canada, it was especially so in Montreal, Quebec which hosted Expo '67 as the World's Fair that year was named. The theme was "Man and His World." The main fair site was on St. Helen's Island opposite downtown Montreal in the St. Lawrence River.

Motor Vessel CANADIAN ENTERPRISE

OWNER:	Upper Lakes Group, Inc.
BUILT:	Port Weller Dry Docks, St. Catharines, Ontario - 1979
HULL NO.:	65
O. A. DIMENSIONS:	730' x 75'8" x 46'6"

This self-unloader utilized the usual word CANADIAN in keeping with the fleet theme and the word ENTERPRISE to specifically refer to the large, then-new contract the fleet had signed with Ontario Hydro for the movement of western coal from Thunder Bay, Ontario to various lower lake plants of the provincial utility.

Enterprise may be defined as "a systematic purposeful activity." This carrier was constructed because of the need for additional self-unloader carrying capacity in light of this new Ontario Hydro contract. While the vessel is not singularly dedicated to this coal trade, its original purpose was to service that additional business.

The Motor Vessel CANADIAN ENTERPRISE sailed on its maiden voyage in December 1979. It is shown in this photograph while enroute on that trip from Conneaut, Ohio to Nanticoke, Ontario with a cargo of coal.

Steamer CANADIAN LEADER

OWNER:	Upper Lakes Group, Inc.
BUILT:	Collingwood Shipyards, Collingwood, Ontario - 1967
HULL NO.:	188
O. A. DIMENSIONS:	730' x 75' x 39'8"
FORMER DATA:	Launched as FEUX FOLLETS. Given present name in 1972.

This bulk freight vessel was the flagship and largest carrier in the Great Lakes fleet of Papachristidis Company Limited before the entire fleet was sold to this owner on March 16, 1972. The ship's former name referred to a ballet group in Montreal, Quebec.

On its maiden voyage the ship sailed from Collingwood in ballast on October 12, 1967 to Port Arthur, Ontario to load grain for a St. Lawrence port.

In this fleet, the ship had no specific namesake. Rather, it carries on a theme of names wherein the first word honors the fact that it is Canadian-owned and operated. The second word of the ship name does not refer to any specific leader, but to all people and things in this general category as a whole.

Since formation, the Upper Lakes family has been a LEADER in the Canadian shipping industry. As such, the name could be said to reflect on the company's own history. The steamer is shown while downbound in the West Neebish Channel, St. Mary's River, on August 7, 1982.

Steamer CANADIAN MARINER

OWNER:	Upper Lakes Group, Inc.
BUILT:	Saint John Shipbuilding and Dry Dock Company, Saint John, New Brunswick - 1963
HULL NO.:	1048
O. A. DIMENSIONS:	731' x 75'3" x 39'3"
FORMER DATA:	Launched as NEWBRUNSWICKER. Renamed GRANDE HERMINE in 1967. Given present name in 1972.

The bulk freight Steamer CANADIAN MARINER set a new Great Lakes wheat cargo record in her initial season of operation. This occurred on September 17th when the ship took onboard 918,215 bushels at Fort William, Ontario for delivery to Montreal, Quebec. The record was surpassed in 1964 by another carrier.

The steamer also set a new soybean cargo record. That happened on June 18, 1965 when it cleared Duluth/Superior Harbor with 885,700 bushels for St. Lawrence River delivery. This record stood until October 18, 1967.

Using the familiar fleet first word, this namesake reference is to all mariners and their trades within and outside the area of the Great Lakes. A definition of a mariner is "one who navigates or assists in navigation, such as a sailor, wheelsman or mate."

The CANADIAN MARINER is shown passing downbound in the West Neebish Channel, St. Mary's River, on May 16, 1982.

Motor Vessel CANADIAN MINER

OWNER:	Upper Lakes Group, Inc.
BUILT:	Canadian Vickers Shipyards, Limited, Montreal, Quebec - 1966
HULL NO.:	287
O. A. DIMENSIONS:	730' x 75' x 39'1"
FORMER DATA:	Launched as MAPLECLIFFE HALL. Given present name in 1994.

On its maiden voyage, this carrier departed Pointe Noire, Quebec on May 1, 1966 with a cargo of iron ore pellets for delivery to Cleveland, Ohio.

This motor vessel utilized the common ULS prefix, CANADIAN, in the vessel name and, specifically, referenced the long history of the MINER in Canada. From zinc, copper, lead and numerous other minerals found in Canada, to the more modern era of "those who mine," the miners in all realms of the mining industry are honored.

If one area of mining was to be singled out for specific reference, it would probably be that of Labrador and Quebec whose iron ore shipments began in 1954 and whose tonnages have been of great value to the St. Lawrence Seaway and the fleets that travel therein.

The Motor Vessel CANADIAN MINER is shown in this photograph being loaded with grain at the Saskatchewan Pool Elevator # 7B at Thunder Bay, Ontario on July 21, 1997.

Motor Vessel CANADIAN NAVIGATOR

OWNER:	Upper Lakes Group, Inc.
BUILT:	J. Readhead & Sons Limited, South Shields, England - 1967
HULL NO.:	619-So. Shields and 66 - Port Weller
O. A. DIMENSIONS:	729'10" x 75'9" x 40'5"
FORMER DATA:	Launched as DEMETERTON. Lengthened 80' at Nederlandsche Dok en Scheepsbouw Maatschappij, Amsterdam, The Netherlands in 1969. Renamed ST. LAWRENCE NAVIGATOR in 1975. Lengthened 82'10" at Port Weller Dry Docks, St. Catherines, Ontario and given present name in 1980. Converted to a self-unloader at the same yard in 1997.

After serving in the ULS Fleet from 1975 through 1979 as a combination saltwater-Great Lakes bulk freighter, the 1980 conversion/lengthening made the vessel strictly suitable for Great Lakes service. The namesake reference uses the familiar first word, denoting a Canadian, and honors all navigators of our Inland Seas.

High demand for self-unloader capacity led these owners to make the 1997 conversion. Number of cargo holds was reduced to three and the self-unloading system is a blend of the hopper-type and the reclaimer-style onboard vessels in the fleet.

The Motor Vessel CANADIAN NAVIGATOR is shown in the photograph above while downbound between Locks No. 7 and No. 6 of the Welland Shop Canal with coal from Conneaut, Ohio for delivery to the Lakeview Plant of Ontario Energy on April 29, 1999.

Motor Vessel CANADIAN OLYMPIC

OWNER:	Upper Lakes Group, Inc.
BUILT:	Port Weller Dry Docks, St. Catharines, Ontario - 1976
HULL NO.:	60
O. A. DIMENSIONS:	730' x 75' x 46'6"

The self-unloading Motor Vessel CANADIAN OLYMPIC was so named because it began life on the Great Lakes in the year in which Montreal, Quebec was the host city for the 1976 Summer Olympic Games. The carrier is a maximum-size Seaway vessel and was this fleet's contribution to expansion of Canadian freighters in 1976. Mr. John D. Leitch, company chairman, felt it apropos to honor the Olympics in naming this ship.

The origin of the Olympic Games dates back to the Greeks, who in 776 B.C. began them as a national festival. Foreigners from many lands were attracted to the festivities. Every four years, the games were held on the plain of Olympia. Under Roman influence the games deteriorated and were finally abolished in 394 A.D. Not until Baron de Coubertin of France inspired revival of the games in 1896 were they promoted again.

Canadians participated for the first time in 1900 when George Orton honored his country by winning a gold medal in the steeplechase. The 1976 Olympics were another triumph for Canada, though financially disturbing. The ship honoring this event is shown while upbound with coal for Thunder Bay, Ontario in the Middle Neebish Channel, St. Mary's River, on May 29, 1977.

Motor Vessel CANADIAN PROGRESS

OWNER:	Upper Lakes Group, Inc.
BUILT:	Port Weller Dry Docks, St. Catharines, Ontario - 1968
HULL NO.:	48
O. A. DIMENSIONS:	730' x 75' x 46'6"

When the self-unloading Motor Vessel CANADIAN PROGRESS was placed in service, it embodied state-of-the-art technology. It was also the first Great Lakes self-unloader for this fleet to be constructed with all accommodations aft. The CANADIAN CENTURY, completed just one year earlier, had the traditional pilot house forward of the cargo hold.

The namesake reference is to the Canadian motto for its centennial year of 1967. That motto was "A Century of Progress." Mr. Leitch, chairman of this fleet, felt it appropriate to utilize the phrase in naming this carrier.

This self-unloader has a single belt gravity system with a reclaiming machine and inclined belt elevator in its cargo hold. The length of the single cargo compartment is 570'. The vessel is built to Lloyds Register of Shipping 100A1 class.

The Motor Vessel CANADIAN PROGRESS is shown while upbound on "The Level" of the Welland Ship Canal on November 22, 1987. In 1970, it set a Great Lakes record for a cargo of barley when it took onboard 1,163,223 bushels at Thunder Bay, Ontario. It sailed on its maiden trip August 24, 1968 from Conneaut, Ohio to Toronto with coal.

Motor Vessel CANADIAN PROSPECTOR

OWNER:	Upper Lakes Group, Inc.
BUILT:	Short Brothers Limited, Sunderland, England - 1964
HULL NO.:	542
O. A. DIMENSIONS:	730' x 75'6" x 42'
FORMER DATA:	Launched as CARLTON. Lengthened 80' at Nederlandsche Dok en Scheepsbouw Maatschappij, Amsterdam, The Netherlands in 1968. Renamed ST. LAWRENCE PROSPECTOR in 1975. Lengthened 88' with new forebody, widened 1'8" and given present name at Saint John Shipbuilding and Dry Dock Company Limited, Saint John, New Brunswick in 1979.

When this vessel came into service for this fleet in 1975, it was a partial answer to the then pressing problem of not enough Canadian vessels for both domestic and foreign transport on the Great Lakes. It served on the Great Lakes during the normal season, then on the oceans during the winter months. As foreign trade dwindled and domestic trade grew, however, it was decided to forego the ocean capability and make the carrier solely a Great Lakes vessel. The conversion noted provided a whole new hull forward of the pilot house and living quarters.

There is no specific namesake intended. The first word is in the fleet's theme and the word PROSPECTOR is a carryover from the vessel's previous name. A prospector may be defined as "one who penetrates into or ranges over for the purpose of geographical or geological discovery." The ship is shown in West Neebish Channel, St. Mary's River, while downbound with grain on June 12, 1981.

Steamer CANADIAN PROVIDER

OWNER:	Upper Lakes Group, Inc.
BUILT:	Collingwood Shipyards, Collingwood, Ontario - 1963
HULL NO.:	177
O. A. DIMENSIONS:	730' x 75'3" x 39'2"
FORMER DATA:	Launched as MURRAY BAY (3). Given present name in 1994.

The bulk freight Steamer CANADIAN PROVIDER was one of eight such vessels acquired by ULS upon the dissolution of an operating company known as Great Lakes Bulk Carriers in April 1994. The firm had its headquarters in St. Catharines, Ontario until it was disbanded.

"GLBC," as it was popularly known, was not unlike Seaway Bulk Carriers which was the joint venture company between ULS and Algoma Central formed in 1990. Unlike the latter company, however, GLBC was short-lived. Owners of vessels pooled into GLBC continued their ownerships and GLBC became the operating company for the purposes of marketing and general supervision.

Using their usual prefix, ULS managers had in mind one of the definitions of the word provide when this name was chosen. One definition which suits is, "to supply something for sustenance or support." Such reference is frequently made to harvests of the field. Surely, Canadian harvests over the years have been quite valuable as PROVIDERs to the world's food supply.

The Steamer CANADIAN PROVIDER is shown passing upbound in the Middle Neebish Channel, St. Mary's River, enroute from Hamilton, Ontario to Thunder Bay, Ontario to load grain on June 23, 1996.

Motor Vessel CANADIAN RANGER

OWNER:	Upper Lakes Group, Inc.
BUILT:	Schlieker-Werft, Hamburg, Germany - 1961
HULL NO.:	43
O. A. DIMENSIONS:	730' x 75' x 39'3"
FORMER DATA:	Launched as GRANDE RONDE at Kaiser Company, Inc., Portland, Oregon in 1943. Renamed KATE N. L. in 1948. Rebuilt by lengthening 203'6", widening with new midbody, converting to a bulk freighter and renaming HILDA MARJANNE at Schlieker-Werft, Hamburg, Germany in 1961. Rebuilt with stern of M.V. CHIMO and given present name at Port Weller Dry Docks, St. Catharines, Ontario in 1984. Converted to a modified self-unloader at Hamilton Marine Division, Canadian Shipbuilding & Engineering Limited, Hamilton Ontario in 1988.

The bulk freight Motor Vessel CANADIAN RANGER utilizes the first word of its name from the fleet theme of names. The RANGER designates no specific ranger, but all "forest keepers" in general.

Like the CANADIAN EXPLORER, this vessel's power plant needed replacing by 1983. Therefore, the stern of the noted vessel was severed and placed on the hull of this carrier. As to the 1988 modification, this was done to accommodate a long term floating contract with Cargill to service their Quebec City, Quebec facility. The boom shown is structurally suited for grain or other light products only.

The carrier is shown loading grain at Saskatchewan Pool Elevator No. 7A at Thunder Bay, Ontario on November 21, 1989.

Motor Vessel CANADIAN TRADER

OWNER:	Upper Lakes Group, Inc.
BUILT:	Davie Shipbuilding, Limited, Lauzon, Quebec - 1969
HULL NO.:	667
O. A. DIMENSIONS:	730' x 75' x 39'8"
FORMER DATA:	Launched as OTTERCLIFFE HALL. Renamed ROYALTON (2) in 1983. Renamed OTTERCLIFFE HALL, for the second time, in 1985. Renamed PETER MISENER in 1988. Given present name in 1994.

The word TRADER conjures up thoughts of the trading world, be it in commodities or stocks and bonds for short term gain. It also applies to ships engaged in the coastal or foreign trades, and such is the reference in this namesake.

The usual prefix, CANADIAN, is used again as the fleet's distinguishing characteristic name, along with TRADER in the context just explained.

It is interesting to note that this vessel established a Great Lakes cargo record for soyabeans in its first season of operation. It loaded 912,527 bushels in Toledo, Ohio on October 18, 1969 for delivery to Baie Comeau, Quebec.

The Motor Vessel CANADIAN TRADER is shown in this photograph just below Lock 8 in the Welland Ship Canal on August 23, 1998. Note the water sprays on deck to help alleviate hogging of the vessel. This is typically done on hot days while traversing the canal.

Motor Vessel CANADIAN TRANSFER

OWNER:	Upper Lakes Group, Inc.
BUILT:	Great Lakes Engineering Works, Ashtabula, Ohio - 1943
HULL NO.:	524
O. A. DIMENSIONS:	650'6" x 60' x 35'
FORMER DATA:	Launched as the powered bulk freighter J. H. HILLMAN, JR. Converted to a self-unloader and renamed CRISPIN OGLEBAY (2) at American Ship Building Company, Toledo, Ohio in 1974. Converted to a bulk freight self-unloading crane-equipped barge at Port Weller Dry Docks, St. Catharines, Ontario and renamed HAMILTON TRANSFER in 1995. Reconverted to a powered self-unloader with stern of CANADIAN EXPLORER, lengthened 30' and given present name at Port Weller Dry Docks, St. Catharines, Ontario in 1998.

The Motor Vessel CANADIAN TRANSFER went into operation in this configuration in the summer of 1998 after having served as a crane-equipped self-unloading barge moored at the DOFASCO steel complex for two years in Hamilton, Ontario harbor.

The 1995 acquisition of the carrier and its use as a barge was necessitated by the collapse of a large unloading tower at DOFASCO'S plant which had regularly been used to unload lake vessels. The cranes were used to dig iron ore pellets from vessels and transfer into the unit's self-unloading system so that they could be placed more quickly on the ore dock. When a new tower was erected, the need for such a TRANSFER disappeared.

The ship is shown in this photograph inbound with limestone at Cleveland, Ohio on August 30, 1998. The Tugs IDAHO and DELAWARE are assisting.

Motor Vessel CANADIAN TRANSPORT

OWNER:	Upper Lakes Group, Inc.
BUILT:	Port Weller Dry Docks, St. Catharines, Ontario - 1979
HULL NO.:	64
O. A. DIMENSIONS:	730' x 75'8" x 46'6"

The Motor Vessel CANADIAN TRANSPORT was the first of two nearly identical ships built for this fleet in 1979. Each was slightly greater in capacity and more sophisticated in design than the CANADIAN OLYMPIC brought out in 1977. A signing of a long term contract between this fleet and Ontario Hydro provided the stimulus for this construction. The cargo hold cubic of this carrier is modestly greater than that of the CANADIAN ENTERPRISE. Both vessels, however, share the same self-unloading equipment. A single belt gravity system with reclaiming machine and a loop belt elevator provide a discharge rate of about 6,000 tons per hour.

Besides utilization of the fleet theme first word, this vessel's specific reference in the second word is to the TRANSPORT of Ontario Hydro's coal, both western from Thunder Bay, Ontario and eastern from various Lake Erie ports to the utility's generating stations.

The Motor Vessel CANADIAN TRANSPORT sailed on its maiden voyage April 19, 1979 and immediately went into Ontario Hydro's coal movement service from the upper lakes.

The carrier is shown while downbound with western coal in the West Neebish Channel, St. Mary's River, on July 20, 1988.

Motor Vessel CANADIAN VENTURE

OWNER:	Upper Lakes Group, Inc.
BUILT:	Davie Shipbuilding, Limited, Lauzon, Quebec - 1965
HULL NO.:	651
O. A. DIMENSIONS:	730' x 75' x 39'2"
FORMER DATA:	Launched as LAWRENCECLIFFE HALL (2). Renamed DAVID K. GARDINER in 1988. Given present name in 1994.

The Motor Vessel CANADIAN VENTURE was constructed and placed in operation at a time when the demand for Canadian vessels of maximum St. Lawrence Seaway size was great. A total of eight new bulk freighters and self-unloaders joined the Canadian fleet in 1965.

ULS Corporation and Algoma Central Marine established a joint venture to market their respective bulk freighter fleets in January 1990. That was the navigation season in which the full impact of two million gross tons of westbound iron ore through the St. Lawrence Seaway would be felt. This was "new business" to supplant ore from two closed land-based mines, and ULS needed additional bulk freight tonnage to handle the movement. Since Algoma had more bulk freight capacity than it needed, the marriage of the two fleets for operating purposes only made a great deal of sense. Ownership of each firm's respective carriers remained in their control. The name chosen for the joint venture was Seaway Bulk Carriers. The VENTURE has rewarded both firms handsomely.

The Motor Vessel CANADIAN VENTURE is shown below passing downbound on "the level," Welland Ship Canal on May 12, 1995 with grain from Toledo, Ohio destined for Baie Comeau, Quebec.

Steamer CANADIAN VOYAGER

OWNER:	Upper Lakes Group, Inc.
BUILT:	Collingwood Shipyards, Collingwood, Ontario - 1963
HULL NO.:	172
O. A. DIMENSIONS:	730' x 75' x 39'2"
FORMER DATA:	Launched as BLACK BAY. Given present name in 1994.

In its initial season of operation, this carrier established two cargo records. One was for iron ore through the St. Lawrence Seaway which amounted to 24, 457 gross tons. The other record was for a full cargo of oats which totaled 1,383,922 U.S. bushels. Both records were broken by other vessels the following season.

The CANADIAN VOYAGER was in a run-down condition when bought by Upper Lakes. It had laid idle at Montreal, Quebec for several seasons prior to 1994. Drydocking and inspection requirements had to be met if the ship was to operate again. Management decided to go forward with repairs. These were accomplished during 1995 in order for the carrier to sail that fall.

Utilizing the familiar CANADIAN as the prefix, the specific namesake reference was to "one who travels by other than land modes." In this case, the ship and its compliment of sailors were all "voyagers."

The steamer is shown while downbound in the West Neebish Channel, St. Mary's River, on July 31, 1997 with a cargo of grain for St. Lawrence River delivery.

Motor Vessel GORDON C. LEITCH (2)

OWNER:	Upper Lakes Group, Inc.
BUILT:	Canadian Vickers Shipyards, Limited, Montreal, Quebec - 1968
HULL NO.:	293
O. A. DIMENSIONS:	730' x 75' x 42'
FORMER DATA:	Launched as the combination self-unloader and bulk freighter RALPH MISENER. Converted to a bulk freighter at Canadian Vickers Shipyards, Limited, Montreal, Quebec in 1977. Given present name in 1994.

Mr. Gordon Clifford Leitch was the founder and first president of ULS Corporation. He was born in Ridgetown, Ontario on February 25, 1893 and was educated in local schools. He began working as the operator of a lumber business, but went to Winnipeg, Manitoba in 1921 to take up the profession of a grain broker with the Manitoba Wheat Pool.

In 1927, Mr. Leitch moved to Toronto, Ontario to become president of Toronto Elevators Company. He formed the Upper Lakes & St. Lawrence Transportation Company and purchased his first vessel, the Steamer SARNIAN, in 1931. He served as president of the shipping line until his death in Toronto on June 2, 1954. At that time, his son, John D. Leitch, succeeded him as the majority owner and president of the company.

The Motor Vessel GORDON C. LEITCH (2) came into this ownership in April 1994. It is shown in this photograph awaiting passage above Lock 7, Welland Ship Canal, on July 9, 1998.

Steamer MONTREALAIS

OWNER: Upper Lakes Group, Inc.
BUILT: Canadian Vickers Shipyards, Limited, Montreal, Quebec - 1962
HULL NO.: 278
O. A. DIMENSIONS: 730' x 75' x 39'
FORMER DATA: Launched as MONTREALER. Given present name in 1962.

The Steamer MONTREALAIS was the first bulk freight vessel ever built for Great Lakes service by its former owner, Papachristidis Company Limited of Montreal, Quebec. The firm had a fleet of ocean-going freighters, but had never operated in the Great Lakes until 1962. After a decade of such operation, the entire fleet of five bulk freighters was sold to this owner.

Mr. Phrixos Basil Papachristidis chose this name to honor the city in which he conducted his shipping empire. He had become known as the "Canadian Greek ship owner" of all of Canada. When Upper Lakes acquired the fleet, they chose not to rename this carrier,

The namesake city is the largest city in Canada and the second largest French-speaking city in the world, behind only Paris, France.

The Steamer MONTREALAIS is shown passing downbound in the West Neebish Channel, St. Mary's River, on June 27, 1982.

Steamer JAMES NORRIS

OWNER:	Upper Lakes Group, Inc.
BUILT:	Midland Shipyards, Midland, Ontario - 1952
HULL NO.:	35
O. A. DIMENSIONS:	663'6" x 67' x 35'
FORMER DATA:	Launched as a bulk freighter. Converted to a self-unloader at Port Weller Dry Docks, St. Catharines, Ontario in 1981.

Mr. James Norris was a man of many interests. He was born in Montreal, Quebec on December 10, 1878 and was educated at McGill University. He came to the United States in 1898 and became a naturalized citizen in 1919.

Mr. Norris formed the Norris Grain Company in Chicago, Illinois in 1906 and was president of the firm from 1908 until his death. In the grain trade on the Great Lakes, he became familiar with Mr. Gordon C. Leitch who interested him in becoming a partner in his fleet, then known as the Upper Lakes and St. Lawrence Transportation Company. The mutual interest each had in ships and the fleet lasted for their lifetimes. Until late 1971, the Norris family maintained a close affiliation with this fleet.

The Steamer JAMES NORRIS was the first newly-built vessel for Upper Lakes. Though they had owned and managed numerous vessels, they had not built one from the keel up. The steamer is shown while upbound in the Welland Ship Canal on July 6, 1997.

Steamer QUEBECOIS

OWNER:	Upper Lakes Group, Inc.
BUILT:	Canadian Vickers Shipyards Limited, Montreal, Quebec - 1963
HULL NO.:	280
O. A. DIMENSIONS:	730' x 75' x 39'

The bulk freight Steamer QUEBECOIS retains a name originally given by Mr. Papachristidis when he had the vessel built. The name honors the people of the Province of Quebec and this owner did not see fit to change it because of the importance of the province to its transportation logistics and cargo origination. The name comes from the French translation of the English word Quebecer, meaning a resident of the province or of Quebec City.

A few salient points about Quebec history are noted here for reference. It was set upon by white men in 1534 when Jacques Cartier landed on the Gaspe Peninsula. The first settlement was made by Champlain at Quebec City in 1608. Montreal was founded by Sieur de Massionneuve in 1642. The area entered Confederation in 1867 as the Province of Quebec. Iron ore was disconvered in Ungava in 1937-1938 and was first shipped from the port of Sept-Iles in 1954. Shipments continue today from Sept-Iles and Pointe Noire across Seven Islands Bay and from Port Cartier.

The Steamer QUEBECOIS is shown passing upbound above Lock No. 3 of the Welland Ship Canal on October 4, 1981.

Steamer SEAWAY QUEEN

OWNER:	Upper Lakes Group, Inc.
BUILT:	Port Weller Dry Docks, St. Catharines, Ontario - 1959
HULL NO.:	25
O. A. DIMENSIONS:	717'3" x 72' x 37'

Upper Lakes commissioned this bulk freghter the year that the modern St. Lawrence Seaway was officially opened. The carrier was named in honor of both the new SEAWAY and the fact that it was the new flagship and QUEEN of the Upper Lakes Fleet.

The St. Lawrence Seaway is controlled 73% by the St. Lawrence Seaway Authority at Cornwall, Ontario and 27% by The Saint Lawrence Seaway Development Corporation at Massena, New York. The sites noted are the operations headquarters. The corporate headquarters for each group are in Ottawa, Ontario and Washington, D.C., respectively.

There was some doubt in the minds of Upper Lakes management as to whether this bulk freighter should be retained into the 21st century since it is not of maximum Seaway size. Upon a full survey of its condition, however, such doubts were dispelled as the vessel was found to be in excellent operating condition. It has, therefore, been put in class for continued operation. The steamer is shown here while downbound in the West Neebish Channel, St. Mary's River, on July 3, 1978.

Barge JOSEPH H. THOMPSON

OWNER:	Upper Lakes Towing Company
BUILT:	Sun Shipbuilding and Dry Dock Company, Chester, Pennsylvania - 1944
HULL NO.:	342
O. A. DIMENSIONS:	706'6" x 71'6" x 38'6"
FORMER DATA:	Launched as the powered C-4 type troop carrier MARINE ROBIN. Rebuilt, lengthened 199'3", Converted to a bulk freighter and given present name at Maryland Drydock Company, Baltimore, Maryland in 1952. Shortened 7'9" and converted to a self-unloading bulk freight barge at Upper Lakes Towing Company, Menominee, Michigan in 1990.

Part of the stern section of this former steamer was used to create a 7,500 shaft horsepower tug, the JOSEPH H. THOMPSON, JR., which pushes the vessel in all but the tightest waters. The tug/barge is shown while inbound at Duluth, Minnesota on July 18, 1997.

The dimensions shown above are those of the combined unit when in its normal operating condition.

Namesake of this carrier was Mr. Joseph Hamilton Thompson who was born in Nashville, Tennessee on October 29, 1900. He graduated from Notre Dame University and served several financial institutions in Cleveland, Ohio before joining the M. A. Hanna Company in 1937 as vice president. He was named president of Hanna in 1952 and became chairman of the board in 1960, serving through 1966. He died in Cleveland on April 30, 1968.

Steamer ARTHUR M. ANDERSON

OWNER:	USS Great Lakes Fleet, Inc.
BUILT:	American Ship Building Company, Lorain, Ohio - 1952
HULL NO.:	868
O. A. DIMENSIONS:	767' x 70' x 36'
FORMER DATA:	Launched as a bulk freighter. Lengthened 120' at Fraser Shipyards, Inc., Superior, Wisconsin in 1975. Converted to a self-unloader at Fraser Shipyards, Inc., Superior, Wisconsin in 1982.

When the Steamer ARTHUR M. ANDERSON took his name, Mr. Arthur Marvin Anderson was a director of United States Steel Corporation, member of its finance committee and vice chairman of J. P. Morgan & Company.

Mr. Anderson was born October 17, 1880 in East Orange, New Jersey and was educated in the public schools. He began his financial career with the investment firm of Libby & Struthers and became a partner there by 1914 when he left to join J. P. Morgan & Company. He was elected a partner in 1926 and vice chairman in 1940 when the firm was incorporated. He was elected to the advisory council in 1959 when the firm was merged to form Morgan Guaranty & Trust Company and held that post when he died on August 10, 1966.

This vessel sailed on its maiden trip August 10, 1952 from Lorain, Ohio in ballast to Two Harbors, Minnesota to load iron ore. It is shown while downbound in the West Neebish Channel, St. Mary's River, on July 3, 1993.

Motor Vessel ROGER BLOUGH

OWNER:	USS Great Lakes Fleet, Inc.
BUILT:	American Ship Building Company, Lorain, Ohio - 1972
HULL NO.:	900
O. A. DIMENSIONS:	858' x 105' x 41'6"

The Motor Vessel ROGER BLOUGH is shown while passing downbound in the West Neebish Channel, St. Mary's River, on July 27, 1996. It had sailed on its maiden trip June 15, 1972 in ballast from Lorain, Ohio to Two Harbors, Minnesota to load iron ore pellets. When commissioned, it was the largest vessel built entirely on the Great Lakes.

Namesake of this self-unloader was Mr. Roger Blough who was born January 19, 1904 in Riverside, Pennsylvania. He was educated at Susquehanna University and Yale University from which he graduated in 1931 with an L1.B. degree.

He practiced law with White & Case from 1931 until 1942 when he became general solicitor of United State Steel Corporation. In 1952, he was elected vice chairman, a director and member of the finance committee. He became chairman of the board on May 3, 1955 and retained that post until retiring January 31, 1969. He died on October 8, 1985 in Hawley, Pennsylvania.

His namesake was built to the greatest dimensions available in 1972, except that it could have been built deeper. That would have allowed its lengthening when larger drydocks were available.

Motor Vessel CALCITE II

OWNER:	USS Great Lakes Fleet, Inc.
BUILT:	American Ship Building Company, Lorain, Ohio—1929
HULL NO.:	804
O. A. DIMENSIONS:	604′9″ × 60′ × 32′
FORMER DATA:	Launched as the bulk freighter WILLIAM G. CLYDE. Converted to a self-unloader at Manitowoc Shipbuilding, Incorporated, Manitowoc, Wisconsin and given present name in 1961.

The Motor Vessel CALCITE II is the second ship to use the name Calcite in the United States Steel Corporation fleet. A former self-unloader was known as the Steamer CALCITE. This vessel has now been scrapped. The Roman numeral II indicates the carry-forward usage of the name.

Calcite, Michigan is the namesake of this self-unloader. It is the largest limestone quarry in the world and is adjacent to United States Steel's shipping and port facilities at Rogers City, Michigan on the western shore of Lake Huron about sixty-five miles below the Straits of Mackinac.

The limestone layers of this property were deposited during the Devonian period of geologic time. It is limestone of high calcium and of unusual purity compared to ordinary limestone. More than fifteen million net tons of this limestone are shipped annually from the Calcite quarry. That property's namesake sailed August 15, 1929 on its maiden voyage from Lorain, Ohio, light to Duluth, Minnesota to load iron ore. This ship is shown while entering Cleveland, Ohio on July 10, 1990.

Steamer CASON J. CALLAWAY

OWNER:	USS Great Lakes Fleet, Inc.
BUILT:	Great Lakes Engineering Works, River Rouge, Michigan—1952
HULL NO.:	297
O. A. DIMENSIONS:	767′ × 70′ × 36′
FORMER DATA:	Launched as a bulk freighter. Lengthened 120′ at Fraser Shipyards, Inc., Superior, Wisconsin in 1974. Converted to a self-unloader at Fraser Shipyards, Inc., Superior, Wisconsin in 1982.

Mr. Cason Jewell Callaway was born on November 6, 1894 at LaGrange, Georgia and received his education in attendance at the University of Virginia. He was born to a family which was prominent in the textile business. His father founded Callaway Mills and this man soon took his position in that company, being named its president in 1920. He retired from that post in 1938 when he was forty-three years of age.

Mr. Callaway bought 25,000 acres of land in Harris County, Georgia and established his Blue Springs Plantation there. He devoted his time to finding and demonstrating new crops which would be profitable to raise in Georgia.

He was elected to the board of directors of United States Steel Corporation in 1944 and served on that board until his death on April 12, 1961. His namesake bulk freighter departed Detroit, Michigan on September 16, 1952, light for Duluth, Minnesota to load its initial cargo of iron ore on its maiden voyage. It is shown here passing downbound in the West Neebish Channel, St. Mary's River, on July 15, 1990.

Steamer PHILIP R. CLARKE

OWNER:	USS Great Lakes Fleet, Inc.
BUILT:	American Ship Building Company, Lorain, Ohio—1952
HULL NO.:	867
O. A. DIMENSIONS:	767′ × 70′ × 36′
FORMER DATA:	Launched as a bulk freighter. Lengthened 120′ at Fraser Shipyards, Inc., Superior, Wisconsin in 1974. Converted to a self-unloader at Fraser Shipyards, Inc., Superior, Wisconsin in 1982.

The Steamer PHILIP R. CLARKE is named for Mr. Philip Ream Clarke who was born in Hinsdale, Illinois on June 10, 1889. He attended Beloit College, Beloit, Wisconsin in 1906. He held honorary degrees from Illinois University in 1954 and Lake Forest University in 1960.

Mr. Clarke was a banker all of his life, having begun his career with Farson, Son & Company in 1908 in Chicago, Illinois. He was manager in Chicago for O'Connor & Kahler in the investment business from 1910 to 1913. From 1914 to 1919 he was president and treasurer of Clarke & Company and from 1919 through 1929, president of the Federal Securities Corporation. After serving as president of Central Trust Company from 1929 to 1932, he became president of the National City Bank and Trust Company and served there until 1956, retiring as chairman of the board.

Among his directorships were those in Montgomery Ward & Company, Pure Oil Company and United States Steel Corporation who honored him when this ship was christened. Mr. Clarke was also very active in civic and charitable activities.

This vessel is shown while downbound in the West Neebish Channel, St. Mary's River on June 11, 1990.

Motor Vessel EDWIN H. GOTT

OWNER:	USS Great Lakes Fleet, Inc.
BUILT:	Bay Shipbuilding Corporation, Sturgeon Bay, Wisconsin - 1979
HULL NO.:	718
O. A. DIMENSIONS:	1,004' x 105' x 56'

The Motor Vessel EDWIN H. GOTT was christened at gala festivities on October 31, 1978. It was named in honor of Mr. Edwin Hays Gott who was born February 22, 1908 in Pittsburgh, Pennsylvania. He graduated from Lehigh University in 1929 with a B.S. degree and began his career with Koppers Company as a management trainee. He joined United States Steel Corporation in 1937 as an industrial engineer at its Ohio Works.

He was named assistant general superintendent of the South Works in Chicago, Illinois in 1948 and general manager in 1953. In 1956, he became vice president-steel operations for all of the company. In 1966, he was elected to the board of directors, and on May 31, 1967, was elected U. S. Steel's president. He was elected chairman and chief executive on February 1, 1969 and retained that post until retiring on February 28, 1973. He remained on the board until his death in Pittsburgh on August 28, 1986.

His namesake sailed on its maiden trip February 16, 1979 in ballast from Milwaukee, Wisconsin to Two Harbors, Minnesota to load iron ore pellets. This was the earliest (or latest) maiden trip in Great Lakes shipping history! The GOTT is shown passing downbound in the West Neebish Channel, St. Mary's River, on June 23, 1996.

Steamer JOHN G. MUNSON (2)

OWNER:	USS Great Lakes Fleet, Inc.
BUILT:	Manitowoc Shipbuilding, Incorporated, Manitowoc, Wisconsin—1952
HULL NO.:	415
O. A. DIMENSIONS:	768′3″ × 72′ × 36′
FORMER DATA:	Lengthened 102′ at Fraser Shipyards, Inc., Superior, Wisconsin in 1976.

Mr. John Gephart Munson was born on January 6, 1885 in Bellefonte, Pennsylvania. In 1906 he became associated with New York Continental Jewel Filtration Company as construction superintendent. In 1909 he joined J. G. White Engineering Corporation and was construction superintendent there until 1919. He joined the Michigan Limestone and Chemical Company in 1919 as operating manager and in 1925 became its vice president. In 1928 he was elected president of both Michigan Limestone and its Bradley Transportation Division, serving in that capacity until 1939 when he became vice president in charge of raw materials for the parent United States Steel Corporation. He continued in that post until retiring in 1951. He died March 28, 1952 in Pittsburgh, Pennsylvania.

United States Steel Corporation paid tribute to his many years of service when this ship was christened in his honor. It was then the largest ship of its type on the Great Lakes. The Steamer JOHN G. MUNSON loaded 21, 011 gross tons of limestone at Calcite, Michigan on July 4, 1953 which was a record cargo that stood until 1966 when a larger cargo was carried by a new Canadian self-unloader. This vessel is shown in the West Neebish channel, St. Mary's River on **July 17, 1990.**

Motor Vessel GEORGE A. SLOAN

OWNER:	USS Great Lakes Fleet, Inc.
BUILT:	Great Lakes Engineering Works, River Rouge, Michigan - 1943
HULL NO.:	292
O. A. DIMENSIONS:	620'6" x 60' x 35'
FORMER DATA:	Launched as the bulk freighter HILL ANNEX. Given present name in 1943. Converted to a self-unloader at Fraser Shipyards, Inc., Superior, Wisconsin in 1967.

Mr. George Arthur Sloan was born in Nashville, Tennessee on May 30, 1893 and graduated from Vanderbilt University with an L1.B. degree in 1915 at which time he was also admitted to the Tennessee Bar.

He was prominent in industry and civic affairs in New York City and was president of the International Chamber of Commerce and the Metropolitan Opera when he died in May 1955. When this vessel took his name, he was a director and member of the finance committee of United States Steel Corporation. During the 1940's, he was also president of the Blue Ridge Mutual Fund and the Nutririon Foundation.

His namesake was originally steam-powered, but was repowered in 1985 with a Caterpiller diesel to increase its efficiency and prolong its life as a Great Lakes carrier.

The Motor Vessel GEORGE A. SLOAN is shown while upbound on the St. Clair River on May 1, 1994.

Motor Vessel EDGAR B. SPEER

OWNER:	USS Great Lakes Fleet, Inc.
BUILT:	American Ship Building Company, Lorain, Ohio - 1980
HULL NO.:	908
O. A. DIMENSIONS:	1,004' x 105' x 56'

Namesake of this ore carrier was Mr. Edgar Boyle Speer who was born in Pittsburgh, Pennsylvania on July 28, 1916. He attended Widener College and the University of Pittsburgh before joining United States Steel Corporation in 1938 as a metallurgical observer at Youngstown, Ohio. He progressed in that post and was transferred to the company's Gary Works in 1951 where he began as the assistant division superintendent.

Mr. Speer was named to various other posts until becoming general superintendent of the Fairless Works in 1956. In 1958, he was named general manager of steel operations, then became vice president-steel operations in 1959. He was elected executive vice president-production in 1967 and a member of the board of directors in 1968. He became president in 1969 and chairman of the board in 1973, serving in that capacity until his death in Pittsburgh on October 13, 1979.

His namesake sailed on its maiden trip September 20, 1980 in ballast from Lorain, Ohio to Two Harbors, Minnesota to load iron ore pellets. It is shown while downbound in the West Neebish Channel, St. Mary's River, on May 17, 1992.

Motor Vessel MYRON C. TAYLOR

OWNER:	USS Great Lakes Fleet, Inc.
BUILT:	Great Lakes Engineering Works, River Rouge, Michigan—1929
HULL NO.:	269
O. A. DIMENSIONS:	603′9″ × 60′ × 32′
FORMER DATA:	Launched as a bulk freighter. Converted to a self unloader at Christy Corporation, Sturgeon Bay, Wisconsin in 1956.

Namesake of this vessel is Mr. Myron Charles Taylor who was born at Lyons, New York on January 18, 1874. He graduated with an Ll.B. degree from Cornell University in 1894 and was admitted to the New York Bar. Mr. Taylor practiced law for a few years and was successful at it, but gave up his practice in 1897 to be a trouble-shooter for the textile industry. He also set up mills in New England and in New Jersey.

He was president of Taylor, Armitage & Company, Inc., Lorraine Securities Corporation, Mercantile Corporation, American Tire Fabric Company and several other firms when J. P. Morgan recruited him into the steel industry. Mr. Taylor became chairman of the finance committee of United States Steel Corporation in 1927 and served as such until 1934. Because of his wise advice and counsel during The Depression, he was named chairman of the board of United States Steel in 1932 and served until retiring in 1938. He remained a director of the corporation, however, until his death on May 6, 1959.

His namesake cleared Detroit, Michigan light for Duluth, Minnesota on August 27, 1929 on its maiden trip. It is shown above while inbound at Cleveland, Ohio on May 23, 1990.

INDEX

VESSEL	PAGE

VESSEL PAGE VESSEL PAGE

VESSEL	PAGE

VESSEL	PAGE

VESSEL PAGE